THE DEVILS

BY ELIZABETH EGLOFF

Based on *The Devils,*
by Fyodor Dostoyevsky

DRAMATISTS
PLAY SERVICE
INC.

THE DEVILS
Copyright © 1999, Elizabeth Egloff
ALL RIGHTS RESERVED

CAUTION: Professionals and amateurs are hereby warned that performance of THE DEVILS is subject to a royalty. It is fully protected under the copyright laws of the United States of America, and of all countries covered by the International Copyright Union (including the Dominion of Canada and the rest of the British Commonwealth), and of all countries covered by the Pan-American Copyright Convention, the Universal Copyright Convention, the Berne Convention, and of all countries with which the United States has reciprocal copyright relations. All rights, including professional/amateur stage rights, motion picture, recitation, lecturing, public reading, radio broadcasting, television, video or sound recording, all other forms of mechanical or electronic reproduction, such as CD-ROM, CD-I, DVD, information storage and retrieval systems and photocopying, and the rights of translation into foreign languages, are strictly reserved. Particular emphasis is placed upon the matter of readings, permission for which must be secured from the Author's agent in writing.

The stage performance rights in THE DEVILS (other than first class rights) are controlled exclusively by the DRAMATISTS PLAY SERVICE, INC., 440 Park Avenue South, New York, N.Y. 10016. No professional or non-professional performance of the Play (excluding first class professional performance) may be given without obtaining in advance the written permission of the DRAMATISTS PLAY SERVICE, INC., and paying the requisite fee.

Inquiries concerning all other rights should be addressed to International Creative Management, 40 West 57th Street, New York, N.Y. 10019, Attn: Sara Jane Leigh.

SPECIAL NOTE

Anyone receiving permission to produce THE DEVILS is required (1) to give credit to the Author as sole and exclusive Author of the Play on the title page of all programs distributed in connection with performances of the Play and in all instances in which the title of the Play appears for purposes of advertising, publicizing or otherwise exploiting the Play and/or a production thereof. The name of the Author must appear on a separate line, in which no other name appears, immediately beneath the title and in size of type equal to 50% of the largest, most prominent letter used for the title of the Play. No person, firm or entity may receive credit larger or more prominent than that accorded the Author; and (2) to give the following acknowledgment on the title page of all programs distributed in connection with performances of the Play:

Originally produced in New York by New York Theatre Workshop.

Original Production directed by Garland Wright.

To Garland

THE DEVILS was produced by New York Theater Workshop (James C. Nicola, Artistic Director; Nancy Kassak Diekmann, Managing Director) in New York City in May, 1997. It was directed by Garland Wright; the set design was by Douglas Stein; the costume design was by Susan Hilferty; the lighting design was by James F. Ingalls; the original music and sound were by David Van Tieghem; and the production stage manager was Charles Means. The cast was as follows:

MATRYOSHA	Nathalie Paulding
NICHOLAS STAVROGIN	Bill Camp
SHIGALYOV	Boris McGiver
STEPAN VERKHOVENSKY	Frank Raiter
VIRGINSKY	Ray Anthony Thomas
LIPUTIN	Patricia Kerr
IVAN SHATOV	Christopher McCann
PETER VERKHOVENSKY	Denis O'Hare
DASHA SHATOV	Kali Rocha
KIRILOV	James Colby
MRS. STAVROGIN	Lynn Cohen
MRS. LEMBKE	Randy Danson
JOSEF BLUM	Daniel Oreskes
GOVERNOR LEMBKE	Michael Arkin
MARIE SHATOV	Patrice Johnson

CHARACTERS

NICHOLAS STAVROGIN — former leader of the Gang of Five
PETER VERKHOVENSKY — leader of the Gang of Five

IVAN SHATOV — printer
SHIGALYOV — welder; also plays THIRD DEPT. OFFICER #1
VIRGINSKY — carpenter
STEPAN VERKHOVENSKY — a literature professor, Peter's father
LIPUTIN — accountant; also plays THIRD DEPT. OFFICER #2

MRS. STAVROGIN — Nicholas' mother
DASHA SHATOV — Shatov's sister
MARIE SHATOV — Shatov's wife
KIRILOV — an engineer

GOVERNOR LEMBKE
FIRST LADY MRS. LEMBKE
JOSEF BLUM — Lembke's secretary
MATRYOSHA — a 12 year old girl

TIME
1870.

PLACE
A small city in the Ukraine.

THE DEVILS

ACT ONE

Scene 1

A Russian officer sitting with a little girl on his lap. His name is Nicholas Stavrogin. Her name is Matryosha. She is twelve. She plays with the buttons on his coat.

MATRYOSHA.
   Where did you get that one

STAVROGIN.
   Paris

MATRYOSHA.
   This one's from Berlin
   This one's from Dresden
   This one's from Budapest
   This one's from Lvov
   and this one's from Paris

STAVROGIN.
   Where's this one from

MATRYOSHA.
   I forget

STAVROGIN.
   Well look
(She looks.)

MATRYOSHA.
   I can't tell

STAVROGIN.
   Look harder you little dunce
(She looks harder. Suddenly he grabs her and starts tickling her. She is giggling. He tickles her harder. They are both giggling as:)

MATRYOSHA.
>Nicholas don't
>Nicholas don't
>Nicholas don't

Scene 2

Day. Shigalyov's room. Five men in three chairs sitting around a table, wearing the heaviest coats they've got: Shigalyov, Liputin, Shatov, Virginsky, and Stepan Verkhovensky. They are playing cards.

SHIGALYOV.
>Next thing you know Nicholas Stavrogin blew up the church

VIRGINSKY.
>He blew up the church?

STEPAN VERKHOVENSKY.
>He didn't blow up the church

SHIGALYOV.
>He blew up the church
>Blew it sky-high

STEPAN VERKHOVENSKY.
>He didn't blow it sky-high
>He blew off the back door
>and it wasn't the church it was the RECTORY

SHIGALYOV.
>Same thing

SHATOV.
>What's a rectory

LIPUTIN.
>May we play the game please

STEPAN VERKHOVENSKY.
>It's not the same thing

VIRGINSKY.
>Did he blow up the graveyard

STEPAN VERKHOVENSKY.
   He doesn't even know what a rectory is
VIRGINSKY.
   Did he blow up the graveyard
STEPAN VERKHOVENSKY.
   No he didn't blow up the graveyard
   he blew up the RECTORY
SHATOV.
   What's a rectory
LIPUTIN.
   It's English
   May we play the game please
VIRGINSKY.
   Cholera
   Cholera would run rampant
STEPAN VERKHOVENSKY.
   I talked to his mother
   His mother told me he blew up the rectory
SHIGALYOV.
   That's what I said
STEPAN VERKHOVENSKY.
   The back door of the rectory
SHIGALYOV.
   Bullshit
STEPAN VERKHOVENSKY.
   What did you say
SHIGALYOV.
   Bullshit
STEPAN VERKHOVENSKY.
   Rude rude rude rude rude rude rude
SHIGALYOV. *(Over:)*
   Bullshit Bullshit Bullshit Bullshit Bullshit Bullshit
(Liputin is slamming his shoe on the table again and again.)

LIPUTIN. *(Over:)*
    Shut up Shut up Shut up Shut up SHUT UP
(Silence.)

SHATOV.
    Why would someone want to blow up a church

LIPUTIN.
    Thank you
    Now
    May we go on with the game please

VIRGINSKY.
    Whose deal is it

LIPUTIN.
    It's not mine

SHIGALYOV.
    It's mine

STEPAN VERKHOVENSKY.
    It's Shatov's deal

SHIGALYOV.
    It's not his deal
    He just dealt
    Gimme the cards

(Shigalyov grabs the cards from Liputin, shuffles, cuts, and starts dealing, as:)

SHATOV.
    I don't understand
    Why would Nicholas Stavrogin want to blow up a church
    What did the Church ever do to him

SHIGALYOV.
    What did it do to him
    What did it do to him

SHATOV.
    That's what I said

SHIGALYOV.
    If I was a businessman
    and I did what the Church is doing

LIPUTIN.
> Oh God

VIRGINSKY.
> Somebody stop them

SHIGALYOV.
> If I told you
> to give me your money
> and in return for your money
> all your sins would be forgiven
> and you'd go to Paradise
>
> you'd be stupid to believe me
> not only that but I'd be committing fraud
> You could send me to jail
> You could inform on me to the Government
> You could inform on me to the Third Department
> You could probably have me deported

SHATOV.
> What are you an atheist

SHIGALYOV.
> No I'm not an atheist

SHATOV.
> That sounds like some kind of atheist statement

SHIGALYOV.
> It's from Nicholas Stavrogin

SHATOV.
> Nicholas Stavrogin never said anything like that

SHIGALYOV.
> Nicholas Stavrogin wrote a whole essay
> fifty-five pages
> on the necessity of blowing up religious monuments
> but you didn't read it, did you

SHATOV.
> A church is not a religious monument

SHIGALYOV.
> What is it then

SHATOV.
A church is not a religious monument

SHIGALYOV.
I can't even have a conversation with him
You can't even have a conversation with this guy

VIRGINSKY.
Shigalyov stop it

SHATOV.
Are you calling Nicholas Stavrogin an atheist

SHIGALYOV.
Nicholas Stavrogin is a revolutionary

SHATOV.
Are you calling Nicholas Stavrogin an atheist

SHIGALYOV.
Yes

SHATOV.
Would you say Moses was an atheist

SHIGALYOV.
Moses

VIRGINSKY.
Oh geez

SHATOV.
Moses came down from the mountain and he said
I shall build me a tabernacle

SHIGALYOV.
Give me those cards back

SHATOV.
Nicholas Stavrogin is not an atheist
and you're a liar and a
and a
You're a rumor that's what you are

SHIGALYOV.
What are you talking about

STEPAN VERKHOVENSKY.
  (Rumor-monger)
SHATOV.
  You're a rumor-monger
  And you're a coward too
SHIGALYOV.
  Pig
SHATOV.
  Coward
SHIGALYOV.
  Oink oink
SHATOV.
  Coward
SHIGALYOV.
  Oink oink
SHATOV.
  Cluck cluck
SHIGALYOV.
  Oink oink
SHATOV.
  Cluck cluck
SHIGALYOV.
  Oink oink oink oink
SHATOV.
  Cluck cluck cluck cluck
STEPAN VERKHOVENSKY.
  Taisez-vous
  Taisez-vous
SHIGALYOV.
  Up yours Verkhovensky
STEPAN VERKHOVENSKY.
  Hear that
  You hear the language he uses

SHIGALYOV.
  You're a conceited ass
VIRGINSKY.
  Order
STEPAN VERKHOVENSKY.
  Say that again
SHIGALYOV.
  You're a conceited ass
  and you're too old for politics
  Go home and write your intellectual textbooks why
     don't you
LIPUTIN.
  May we start the game please
  May we start the game please
STEPAN VERKHOVENSKY.
  What's wrong with intellectual
VIRGINSKY.
  Order
LIPUTIN.
  Sit down everybody
VIRGINSKY.
  Order
STEPAN VERKHOVENSKY.
  What's wrong with intellectual I'd like to know
LIPUTIN.
  Sit down
(Virginsky grabs the shoe from Liputin and pounds it on the table.)
VIRGINSKY.
  ORDER ORDER ORDER
(The sound of a glacier shifting overhead. Wood straining. Glass creaking. Silence.)
  It's the Third Department
LIPUTIN.
  They heard everything we said

STEPAN VERKHOVENSKY.
  Oh God oh God oh God
SHIGALYOV.
  Shhhhhhh
(Pause. They listen.)
LIPUTIN.
  Now you've done it
  I knew you'd do it
  We're all going to be arrested
STEPAN VERKHOVENSKY.
  They've got guns
  They're going to put us in the back of a wagon
  and pretend they're driving us to jail
  but they won't
  Instead they'll drive us out to the forest
  and put a bullet in each of our brains
  Five brains
  Five bullets
  and nobody will ever know
SHIGALYOV.
  Shut up Granny
(Footsteps coming down the stairs, coming down the stairs and pausing in front of the door. Slowly the doorknob turns, the door swings open. It's a man. He stands in the doorway with a briefcase. He takes off his hat. His shadow is enormous. It is the student Peter Verkhovensky.)

PETER VERKHOVENSKY.
  Hello everybody sorry I'm late
  Shall we get started?

Scene 3

Back to Stavrogin and Matryosha: instant replay.

MATRYOSHA.
  Where did you get that one

STAVROGIN.
　Paris

MATRYOSHA.
　This one's from Berlin
　This one's from Dresden
　This one's from Budapest
　This one's from Lvov
　and this one's from Paris

STAVROGIN.
　Where's this one from

MATRYOSHA.
　I forget

STAVROGIN.
　Well look
(She looks.)

MATRYOSHA.
　I can't tell

STAVROGIN.
　Look harder you little dunce
(She looks harder. Suddenly he grabs her and starts tickling her. She is giggling. He tickles her harder. They are both giggling as:)

MATRYOSHA.
　Nicholas don't
　Nicholas don't
　Nicholas don't

Scene 4

Back to Shigalyov's room. Peter Verkhovensky stands before the gang, holding up a printing plate.

PETER VERKHOVENSKY.
　This is a printing plate
　There are only 5 of these in the entire country
　Notice the woman
　Freedom

    striding forward into battle
    with a little child at her breast
    and the little child says

STEPAN VERKHOVENSKY.
    What's that in her hand

LIPUTIN.
    That's a potato

SHIGALYOV.
    That's not a potato
    That's an axe

PETER VERKHOVENSKY.
    And the little child says
    Strike

    The little child says Strike
    It's written right there
    next to its mouth

(Pause.)

LIPUTIN.
    Nice Very nice
    and impressive too
    Not everyone gets to print a poster

SHIGALYOV.
    I think the little child should say Fuck you

VIRGINSKY.
    Wait a minute
    Does this mean we're going to do it
    I mean really really do it

PETER VERKHOVENSKY.
    Virginsky we already talked about this

VIRGINSKY.
    Yes but I'm asking Does this mean it's official

PETER VERKHOVENSKY.
    It's an official idea

LIPUTIN.
    This is only a discussion Virginsky

VIRGINSKY.
>   All right then
>   As long as we're only discussing it
(Silence.)

PETER VERKHOVENSKY.
>   Now we'll need a nice thick paper
>   We need to be able to hang this thing all over town
>   Let's make twenty copies

LIPUTIN.
>   Twenty would be fine

PETER VERKHOVENSKY.
>   No Let's make forty copies
>   I know it's a rush
>   but we need it done by tomorrow okay Shatov

VIRGINSKY.
>   I thought this was only a discussion

PETER VERKHOVENSKY.
>   Okay Shatov

SHATOV.
>   What

PETER VERKHOVENSKY.
>   You're the printer
>   Can you do it by tomorrow

SHIGALYOV.
>   Virginsky's scared

VIRGINSKY.
>   Of course I'm scared
>   If you had any brains you'd be scared too

SHIGALYOV.
>   I'm scared but I'm not terrified

LIPUTIN.
>   Virginsky listen
>   A lot of other people are going to print this poster too
>   There are going to be millions of them
>   all over the country

VIRGINSKY.
>   But remember the last guy who printed a poster
>   He hung it on the wall of the hardware store
>   and now he's dead

SHIGALYOV.
>   He's not dead
>   He's in prison

VIRGINSKY.
>   You haven't spoken to him
>   You haven't seen him
>   Nobody's seen him for five years

STEPAN VERKHOVENSKY.
>   And before him there was the other one
>   Whathisname

LIPUTIN.
>   He was a lunatic

VIRGINSKY.
>   Yes but they sentenced him to thirty years hard labor
>   didn't they

PETER VERKHOVENSKY.
>   You're right Virginsky
>   If we print this poster we might get arrested
>   But if we get arrested
>   we'll have lots of company

LIPUTIN.
>   They'll have to arrest the entire country

SHIGALYOV.
>   They'd never dare

PETER VERKHOVENSKY.
>   Questions? Comments anybody?

(Pause.)

LIPUTIN.
>   All right then let's take a vote
>   Somebody make a motion

PETER VERKHOVENSKY.
> I think Shatov has something to say
> Shatov
> Did you want to say something

SHATOV.
> I'll need a new roller

PETER VERKHOVENSKY.
> That's a matter for your group Treasurer

SHATOV.
> I mean a good roller

LIPUTIN.
> Well don't look at me

PETER VERKHOVENSKY.
> Who's the group Treasurer this month

LIPUTIN.
> We don't have a group Treasurer this month
> because nobody wanted to be nominated

SHIGALYOV.
> We don't need a group Treasurer
> because nobody's got any money

VIRGINSKY.
> Liputin's got money

LIPUTIN.
> Why do I have to pay for everything

SHIGALYOV.
> Liputin give Shatov some of your money

LIPUTIN.
> No

SHIGALYOV.
> Liputin

LIPUTIN.
> What about you Virginsky
> Your wife has a job

VIRGINSKY.
Oh for Christ's sake

SHIGALYOV.
She's a WOMAN

PETER VERKHOVENSKY.
Gentlemen
Gentlemen
We're not really arguing about money, are we
(Silence.)

SHIGALYOV.
I just like to know who's going to pay for things

STEPAN VERKHOVENSKY.
May I ask a question

SHATOV.
I think we should talk to Nicholas Stavrogin
about this poster
(Pause.)

SHIGALYOV.
Nicholas Stavrogin's in Berlin you idiot

VIRGINSKY.
I thought he was in Paris

SHATOV.
Nicholas Stavrogin's the leader
I think we should talk to the leader
before we vote

LIPUTIN.
This is ridiculous

STEPAN VERKHOVENSKY.
May I ask a question

SHATOV.
It's not ridiculous
It's the rule

SHIGALYOV.
  What rule
  There's no rule that we have to talk to the leader

STEPAN VERKHOVENSKY.
  Peter Son Son
  May I ask a question

PETER VERKHOVENSKY.
  Yes Dad

STEPAN VERKHOVENSKY.
  About this strike
  I don't see how I can go on strike
  I'm a writer

PETER VERKHOVENSKY.
  Dad
  None of these men has a job
  and yet they've been coming to these meetings for
  what is it two years

LIPUTIN.
  Four

VIRGINSKY.
  Five

PETER VERKHOVENSKY.
  Because they're committed to the future of this country

STEPAN VERKHOVENSKY.
  But we've never had to do anything before now

PETER VERKHOVENSKY.
  So here's your chance
  Shall we take a vote

SHIGALYOV.
  I want to know how long this strike is supposed to last
  Six weeks? Six months?

PETER VERKHOVENSKY.
  It might last six years
  It might last sixty years

LIPUTIN.
>We're talking about changing a system that's been in place for a thousand years

PETER VERKHOVENSKY.
>By the time this strike is over
>you may not have a room and you may not have bread
>You may be living in the gutter
>along with millions of other people
>but together you will rise up from the gutter
>and you will change the course of history

(Pause.)

LIPUTIN.
>Jesus Christ I'll pay for the posters

PETER VERKHOVENSKY.
>Thank you Liputin
>Now shall we vote

SHATOV.
>Nicholas Stavrogin would say this is stupid

PETER VERKHOVENSKY.
>Excuse me Shatov

SHATOV.
>Nicholas Stavrogin would say
>if we put posters in the school
>we'll get the students kicked out
>If we put posters in the factory
>we'll get the workers fired

PETER VERKHOVENSKY.
>Nicholas Stavrogin would also say
>That's how you start a revolution

STEPAN VERKHOVENSKY.
>Yes but Son
>Peter

PETER VERKHOVENSKY.
>Quiet Dad

(Pause.)

LIPUTIN.
　Does anybody want to make a motion
SHIGALYOV.
　I make a motion we print this poster
(Another pause.)
VIRGINSKY.
　I second
LIPUTIN.
　All those in favor raise your hand
(Liputin, Virginsky, and Shigalyov raise their hands.)
　All those against
(Stepan Verkhovensky raises his hand halfway, and puts it down.)
　All those abstaining
(Stepan Verkhovensky raises his hand and keeps it up.)
PETER VERKHOVENSKY.
　Shatov
　Don't you want to vote
SHATOV.
　No
PETER VERKHOVENSKY.
　Why not
SHATOV.
　Because
PETER VERKHOVENSKY.
　Because why
SHATOV.
　Because I don't want to that's why
(Suddenly the door is thrown open. A woman heaves a basket loaded with laundry into the room. She drops it on the floor with a boom. Her name is Dasha. Shatov crosses to her. They whisper.)
SHIGALYOV.
　Why does she always have to bring his laundry to my house
LIPUTIN.
　Excuse me Dasha
　but your brother is in the middle of a meeting

DASHA.
> Don't worry
> I'm not going to spoil your stupid little game
> *(Dasha goes, leaving the laundry basket. Shatov returns to the table.)*

PETER VERKHOVENSKY. *(To Shatov.)*
> Some people will never understand the meaning of revolution
> Some people will never be more than back-water farm-boys
> Let everybody else do the dying, why don't you
> Maybe their blood will fill your belly

(Peter leaves. Liputin starts to follow.)

LIPUTIN. *(To Shatov.)*
> See what you've done
> You've made him mad

SHIGALYOV.
> Come back here Liputin
> *(Liputin comes back, takes out his wallet and drops a bill on the table. Shatov takes it.)*
> Miser

LIPUTIN.
> Intellectual
> *(Liputin slams out the door.)*

VIRGINSKY.
> I think it was a better plan to kill the Tsar

STEPAN VERKHOVENSKY.
> We can't kill the Tsar
> He's in St. Petersburg
> That's four hundred miles away
> We can't even afford train fare

(Pause.)

SHATOV.
> I still think we should wait
> until Nicholas Stavrogin comes back

SHIGALYOV.
> Nicholas Stavrogin's not coming back
> He's never coming back

SHATOV.
>He said he was coming back

SHIGALYOV.
>That was two and a half years ago

STEPAN VERKHOVENSKY.
>His mother came back last night

SHIGALYOV.
>So what

VIRGINSKY.
>Did she find him

SHIGALYOV.
>Nicholas Stavrogin will never be found
>until he wants to be found

STEPAN VERKHOVENSKY.
>Well my friends
>As Monsieur Candide said:
>*Toute est possible dans les meilleurs des mondes*

SHIGALYOV.
>YOU SHUT UP
>Goddamn French

Scene 5

Kirilov's room. Kirilov is a body-builder. Peter Verkhovensky and Liputin watch him holding a pair of dumbbells over his head, and counting.

KIRILOV.
>Forty-four, 45, 46, 47, 48, 49, 50.
>*(He puts the weights down, and reaches for a towel.)*

PETER VERKHOVENSKY.
>That's quite a work-out

LIPUTIN.
>He can do push-ups too

KIRILOV.
    Show Peter how many push-ups you can do
(No response. Kirilov is getting up, and pouring himself a cup of tea.)

PETER VERKHOVENSKY.
    Mister Liputin and I have come because
    the group's plans have reached the point
    where they need to work out an agreement with you

KIRILOV.
    Don't tell me they're actually going to do something

LIPUTIN.
    Shut up

KIRILOV.
    Tea Mister Verkhovensky

PETER VERKHOVENSKY.
    Thank you
(Kirilov pours tea into a second cup.)

KIRILOV.
    I never thought it was good to eat a lot
    I think all one should eat
    is a bit of bread now and then
    vegetables if they're in season

    and tea
    Don't you know
    the worst thing about being abroad
    was getting a good cup of tea

PETER VERKHOVENSKY.
    That's right
    You just came back from abroad, didn't you Kirilov

LIPUTIN.
    Chicago

PETER VERKHOVENSKY.
    That's right Chicago
    I don't think I've heard your side of the story

KIRILOV.
    I don't have a side of the story

LIPUTIN.
>   Just that he screwed up
>   Him and Shatov
>   We had to bail them out after a year and a half

KIRILOV.
>   After we wrote you five times

LIPUTIN.
>   After you spent all our money

KIRILOV.
>   After you only gave us a hundred

LIPUTIN.
>   You were supposed to get JOBS

KIRILOV.
>   There weren't any jobs

(To Peter.)
>   According to Nicholas Stavrogin
>   Chicago
>   was supposed to be a worker's Paradise

LIPUTIN.
>   Oh sure
>   Blame it on Nicholas Stavrogin

KIRILOV.
>   The only thing that bothers me
>   is that I won't live long enough to spit on
>   Nicholas Stavrogin's grave
>   Sugar?

(Kirilov hands Peter a cup of tea.)

PETER VERKHOVENSKY.
>   Yes please

(Peter takes some sugar from the tray, and puts it directly into his mouth. He pours some tea into his saucer and politely slurps it from there. Kirilov follows suit. Liputin pulls a flask out of his jacket, and takes a slug.)
>   So Kirilov
>   You say you're willing to write a letter for the group

KIRILOV.
>   Not for the group
>   But for everybody else For humanity Yes

PETER VERKHOVENSKY.
>   Okay

KIRILOV.
>   And only as long as the Third Department
>   doesn't think I was scared or depressed
>   or pressured into it

LIPUTIN.
>   Big deal

KIRILOV.
>   So what's it going to be
>   A bombing

PETER VERKHOVENSKY.
>   I don't know yet

KIRILOV.
>   Okay Now let's talk about money
>   I figure I deserve to get paid
>   for helping you fellows out
>   How about three hundred

LIPUTIN.
>   Three hundred

PETER VERKHOVENSKY.
>   If you don't mind my asking
>   What does a dead man want with money

KIRILOV.
>   Four hundred

LIPUTIN.
>   Four hundred

KIRILOV.
>   Five hundred is my final offer
>   Five hundred or I won't do it

LIPUTIN.
 Five

PETER VERKHOVENSKY.
 Five hundred is fine
 Is that fine with you, Liputin

LIPUTIN.
 Yeah but
 Okay but what if he backs out

PETER VERKHOVENSKY.
 I don't think Kirilov intends to back out

KIRILOV.
 I'm not going to back out
 I don't give a damn about you or the Society anymore
 The revolution is going to happen with you or without you
 But if my death will move things along a little faster
 that's fine with me

PETER VERKHOVENSKY.
 That's fine with me
 Is that fine with you Liputin

LIPUTIN.
 That's fine with me

KIRILOV.
 Have you got any idea of when you'll be needing me

PETER VERKHOVENSKY.
 Soon
 We'll be in touch

LIPUTIN.
 Shouldn't we have something in writing

PETER VERKHOVENSKY.
 Can I ask you something Kirilov

KIRILOV.
 What

PETER VERKHOVENSKY.
 What makes somebody want to kill himself
(Pause.)

KIRILOV.
  To get free

PETER VERKHOVENSKY.
  Free from what

KIRILOV.
  The fear

LIPUTIN.
  Fear of what

PETER VERKHOVENSKY.
  Fear of what

KIRILOV.
  The fear of pain
  The fear of dying

PETER VERKHOVENSKY.
  That's good

KIRILOV.
  I don't care whether or not you think it's good
(Kirilov gets up and opens the door.)
  Remember:
  Five hundred
  And don't spring it on me, either
  I need a few hours' notice

LIPUTIN.
  If we're paying you to do it, you'll do it

PETER VERKHOVENSKY.
  Thank you Liputin
  Now I'd like to speak to Kirilov alone for a minute
(Liputin goes. Peter nods at the ceiling.)
  Has he had any visitors

KIRILOV.
  Shatov

PETER VERKHOVENSKY.
  I want to know

KIRILOV.
  No

(Peter goes. Outside, Liputin is waiting for him. After Kirilov shuts the door.)

LIPUTIN.
   Don't think I'm going to be the one to pay him
   I haven't got 500

PETER VERKHOVENSKY.
   Shhhh

(Peter is putting his ear to Kirilov's door, and listening. Somewhere in the building, water is dripping. A door slams. Footsteps run down a flight of stairs. Another door slams.)

LIPUTIN.
   So when is it going to be

PETER VERKHOVENSKY.
   When is what going to be

LIPUTIN.
   The thing we're going to do
   The thing Kirilov is going to take the blame for
   The bombing

PETER VERKHOVENSKY.
   I didn't say it was a bombing

LIPUTIN.
   I didn't say it was a bombing either
   Though a bombing would be good
   If that's what you decide to do
   But if you don't want to do a bombing
   That would be good too

(Peter takes his ear away from the door, and hunts for a cigarette.)

PETER VERKHOVENSKY.
   I don't know

LIPUTIN.
   You don't know

PETER VERKHOVENSKY.
   No

LIPUTIN.
   You mean you really don't know

or you mean you know
and I'm not supposed to know

PETER VERKHOVENSKY.
I mean I don't know

LIPUTIN.
I see

PETER VERKHOVENSKY.
I think you'd better get out of here

LIPUTIN.
I don't have to spend my time following you around

PETER VERKHOVENSKY.
Run

(Liputin runs off. Peter steps back into darkness. A moment later, Shatov appears, lugging the laundry basket. Shatov passes Peter, and climbs up a set of dark stairs. At the top of the stairs, he comes to a locked door. He unlocks one, two locks, and pushes the door open. Shatov's room. Through a hole in the roof, sunlight is visible. On the table, a printing press. Shatov drops the laundry basket, and takes out the printing plate, and a roller. As he starts setting up the press, Peter Verkhovensky watches from the dark.)

Scene 6

A society lady, furiously unpacking a trunk. Her name is Mrs. Stavrogin. She is handing everything to Dasha, who is putting it away. Stepan Verkhovensky appears.

STEPAN VERKHOVENSKY.
Welcome home *ma cherie*
How was Berlin

MRS. STAVROGIN.
Must you jump at me Mister Verkhovensky
What are you wearing
Is that a red tie

Don't tell me you're wearing a red tie
at this hour of the day
Stand up straight
Have you been taking your morning constitutional

STEPAN VERKHOVENSKY.
Mais oui

MRS. STAVROGIN.
Five miles

STEPAN VERKHOVENSKY.
Ah non

MRS. STAVROGIN.
I can always tell
I can see it in your face
From now on you'll walk

eight miles a day
Eight
You hear me

STEPAN VERKHOVENSKY.
So tell me: how was Berlin

MRS. STAVROGIN.
Don't mention that city to me
The Germans know absolutely nothing about cuisine
I nearly starved to death while I was there

STEPAN VERKHOVENSKY.
Did you find Nicholas

MRS. STAVROGIN.
I found Nicholas all right
Nicholas
came to visit me at my hotel

The next thing I knew he was arrested
in Munich
passing a check with my signature on it
for six hundred marks

STEPAN VERKHOVENSKY.
Gasp

MRS. STAVROGIN.
> But would he apologize No
> He has no remorse not a drop
> my very own son
>
> *Le beau monsieur sans merci*

STEPAN VERKHOVENSKY.
> *Vraiment*

MRS. STAVROGIN.
> I bailed him out
> Now for all I know
> his body's drifting down the Whatsit

STEPAN VERKHOVENSKY.
> I'm about to be arrested too

MRS. STAVROGIN.
> He broke my heart you know
> when he dropped out of the university
> I have no more love to give him

STEPAN VERKHOVENSKY.
> I'm about to be arrested too

MRS. STAVROGIN.
> Some boys think
> a mother's love is infinite
> It's not true

STEPAN VERKHOVENSKY.
> I'M ABOUT TO BE ARRESTED TOO

MRS. STAVROGIN.
> Ewe?

STEPAN VERKHOVENSKY.
> Three weeks ago I was in receipt of this
> anonymous letter
> *(He produces a letter.)*
> I am
> a corrupter of young people
> an advocate of atheism
>
> and a disseminator of pornography

(As she takes the letter, and reads it, he continues.)
>Of course I can see why they'd call me
>a corrupter of young people
>Back when I was teaching at the university
>
>my theories on 18th century
>colonial history
>raised quite a few hackles
>
>And of course young people have always listened to me
>Far too much
>They give my opinions far too much weight

MRS. STAVROGIN.
>This is why I can't invite
>my friends in Moscow to visit
>In Moscow they have freedom of speech
>In Moscow they have newspapers
>The last time this town had a newspaper was in
>EIGHTEEN FORTY-EIGHT

STEPAN VERKHOVENSKY.
>Unfortunately if he arrests me
>he'll be sure to arrest you too

MRS. STAVROGIN.
>Me

STEPAN VERKHOVENSKY.
>The new Governor
>Didn't I tell you
>We have a new Governor

MRS. STAVROGIN.
>I know we have a new Governor

STEPAN VERKHOVENSKY.
>The new Governor
>is having me followed
>He's hired an actual snoop
>
>The snoop follows me everywhere
>Last Sunday he knocked on the front door
>and started asking me all kinds of questions

About you and me
and what we're doing
living together under the same roof

tous les deux

When I told him you rule the province
he sneered
and said the Governor would put a stop to that

MRS. STAVROGIN.
I never said I rule the province

STEPAN VERKHOVENSKY.
But the fact is
you do
though you're much too humble to say so

MRS. STAVROGIN.
In spirit
more than
actuality

STEPAN VERKHOVENSKY.
Nevertheless
They always go after the intellectuals
first

MRS. STAVROGIN.
Dasha get my carriage

DASHA.
Yes ma'am
(Dasha exits.)

STEPAN VERKHOVENSKY.
Where are you going

MRS. STAVROGIN.
To see the Governor

STEPAN VERKHOVENSKY.
You mustn't

MRS. STAVROGIN.
I must

(Stepan Verkhovensky seizes Mrs. Stavrogin's hand and goes down on one knee. His head is barely visible above the trunk.)

STEPAN VERKHOVENSKY.
> *Che bella!*
>
> You may not be the only intelligent person in the world
> but there are few people
> more intelligent than yourself.

(She exits. He runs after her.)

Scene 7

Shatov exits his room, and goes down the dark stairs. Peter Verkhovensky hides. Shatov passes, descends to Kirilov's door, and taps on it.

SHATOV.
> Kirilov

KIRILOV'S VOICE.
> Who is it

SHATOV.
> Do you have a screwdriver I could borrow
> Or a wrench
> Actually both
> I need a screwdriver and a wrench in order to

(Kirilov throws open the door.)

KIRILOV.
> I TOLD YOU I DON'T WANT TO SPEAK TO YOU
>   EVER AGAIN

(Kirilov slams the door in Shatov's face. Shatov kicks the door.)

SHATOV.
> ATHEIST
> YOU'RE A GODDAMN ATHEIST
> I OUGHT TO TURN YOU IN TO THE THIRD
>   DEPARTMENT

(Shatov gives Kirilov's door another kick, runs back up the stairs, and slams the door. Pause. Peter Verkhovensky steps out of the shadows, and starts climbing the stairs after Shatov.)

Scene 8

The Governor's parlor. Mrs. Stavrogin stands before First Lady Mrs. Lembke. Stepan Verkhovensky and Dasha shrink into the background.

MRS. STAVROGIN.
Madam First Lady I stand before you in my shame
the victim of
accusations contending that

a) I am housing a political subversive
b) I am defaming the corpse
of my patriot husband
by paying said subversive to service me and
c) I am nothing less
than the leader of the intellectual elite

MRS. LEMBKE.
Well I'm impressed
Anyone who can speak as well as you
should certainly be above reproach

MRS. STAVROGIN.
Thank you

MRS. LEMBKE.
Does that mean you aren't
the leader of the intellectual elite

MRS. STAVROGIN.
Madam Lembke
My salons are not and never have been
anything but coffee-klatches for the rich

my friends bathetic
panty-waists and intellectuals
Why we're all devotees

of Romantic art
and as you know that makes us
irrelevant

> in a town like this
> where folks can barely
> spell the word

MRS. LEMBKE.
> Don't I know it
(To Stepan Verkhovensky.)
> And are you the subversive who services her

MRS. STAVROGIN.
> This man is my tutor not my lover

STEPAN VERKHOVENSKY.
> My name is Stepan Verkhovensky

MRS. STAVROGIN.
> I employ this man for educational purposes

MRS. LEMBKE.
> What did you say your name was

STEPAN VERKHOVENSKY.
> My name is Stepan Verkhovensky
> I am the author of the forthcoming "The Golden Age:
> A Complete Compendium of Spanish Literature
> From the 16th and 17th Centuries"

(Mrs. Lembke screams.)

MRS. LEMBKE.
> Do you have a son named Peter Verkhovensky

STEPAN VERKHOVENSKY.
> Yyyyyyes

(She bangs on the wall.)

MRS. LEMBKE.
> ANDREIIIII
> ANDREIIIII
> GET IN HERE THIS MINUTE

(Turning back to Stepan.)
> Ssssuch a fascinating young man
> You must be so proud
> Peter's taught me everything I know about politics
> Why he's the smartest young man in his entire generation

In fact he's coming to my salon today
Sit down Sit down
Have a vodka A chocolate
I always have a salon on Tuesday
This is Tuesday, isn't it

MRS. STAVROGIN.
Madame First Lady
your husband is
planning to have Mister Verkhovensky and myself arrested
(Pause.)

MRS. LEMBKE.
Says who

MRS. STAVROGIN.
Mister Verkhovensky

STEPAN VERKHOVENSKY.
I didn't say

MRS. LEMBKE.
Why in the world would my husband want to arrest you

MRS. STAVROGIN.
That's what I'm asking you

MRS. LEMBKE.
Perhaps it's because of
a certain anonymous letter

STEPAN VERKHOVENSKY and MRS. STAVROGIN.
Anonymous letter
(Mrs. Lembke pulls a letter out of her bosom.)

MRS. LEMBKE.
Which I just received this morning
It's about Mrs. Stavrogin's son
What's his name

MRS. STAVROGIN.
Nicholas

MRS. LEMBKE.
That's him
and his group of anarchists too

MRS. STAVROGIN.
   My son is not an anarchist

MRS. LEMBKE. *(Reading.)*
   Nicholas Stavrogin is an atheist and a murderer
   Arrest the ugly bastard
   as soon as he gets here
   or you'll get your heads sliced off bloody
   Death to the Anarchists

MRS. STAVROGIN.
   For God's sake

MRS. LEMBKE.
   Is your son coming home

MRS. STAVROGIN.
   No of course not

MRS. LEMBKE.
   Then what are you worried about
   This town is full of crack-pots
   I get a letter like this almost every week

   Anyway ladies like us aren't interested
   in who's about to be arrested
   With any luck it won't be us

MRS. STAVROGIN.
   Yes but

MRS. LEMBKE.
   Mrs. Stavrogin This weekend I'm throwing a charity ball
   for more than two hundred people
   including thirty-five members of the intellectual elite
   from St. Petersburg, Moscow, Kiev, you name it

   It's going to be the biggest charity ball
   this side of the Caucasus
   and all in honor of my favorite cause:
   "Russia: A New Beginning"
   You like it?

MRS. STAVROGIN.
   I love it

MRS. LEMBKE.
> Since you're the local *doyenne of savoir faire*
> let's make a deal:
> Help me plan this damn thing
> If your boy shows up
> I'll tell the Governor to go easy on him

MRS. STAVROGIN.
> You mean you won't let your husband deport Nicholas

(Mrs. Lembke tears up the letter.)

MRS. LEMBKE.
> Nicholas
>   will not exist

(She turns to the wall and pounds on it again.)

>   ANDREIIIII WHAT THE HELL IS GOING ON IN THERE

(<u>Go To</u>: the other side of the wall, where two men tear their ears away from a single listening device. They are the Governor, and his secretary, Mister Blum.)

LEMBKE.
> So Nicholas Stavrogin is coming back

BLUM.
> Just as Peter Verkhovensky
> is trying to start a national strike
> I don't suppose it's a coincidence, do you

LEMBKE.
> Do they think we're stupid

BLUM.
> They think we're scared

LEMBKE.
> They think we're going to stand by
> and let them start a national strike
> I could have them arrested for this
> arrested and sent to Siberia
> What are you doing

(Blum is reaching into the Governor's pocket, taking out his wallet, and removing several bills.)

BLUM.
> With your permission sir
> I need to hire some more men

LEMBKE.
> Blum
> Blum
> Blum

(Blum is climbing out the window. He turns back.)

BLUM.
> Yes sir

LEMBKE.
> Don't Get Caught

(Blum exits.)

Scene 9

Peter Verkhovensky knocks on Shatov's door, opens it, and sticks his head in.

PETER VERKHOVENSKY.
> Sorry
> Didn't mean to scare you

SHATOV.
> What do you want

PETER VERKHOVENSKY.
> Just thought I'd come by
> and see how you're doing

SHATOV.
> I'm okay

PETER VERKHOVENSKY.
> Listen you don't have to print the posters you know
> We can get somebody else to do it

SHATOV.
> I'll do it

PETER VERKHOVENSKY.
> That's what you say
> but I have a suspicion you don't want to

SHATOV.
> I'll do it

PETER VERKHOVENSKY.
> It's interesting you know
> Fear
> It's never the fear that's the problem is it
> It's the effect of the fear

SHATOV.
> I'm not afraid

PETER VERKHOVENSKY.
> Of course you are
> We're all afraid
> I'm afraid of you
> and your friends are afraid of me
>
> They're afraid of being hungry
> and they're afraid of getting arrested
> but you're not afraid of those things, are you
>
> You're afraid of what will happen if you vote
> and you're afraid of what will happen if you don't vote
> It's all the same
> It's fear that gets us in the end

(Peter is fiddling with the handle of the printer. Shatov watches him.)

SHATOV.
> If anyone gets arrested it's going to be me

PETER VERKHOVENSKY.
> Actually you're right
> You'll be the first one to get arrested
> and no one will be able to help you
>
> No one will want to help you
> Liputin and Shigalyov and Virginsky and even my father
> They may be your friends
> but they're only human

SHATOV.
>They're not the ones I'm worried about

PETER VERKHOVENSKY.
>Who are the ones you're worried about

SHATOV.
>What do you mean

PETER VERKHOVENSKY.
>In your opinion
>who are the people we should be worrying about

SHATOV.
>The Third Department I guess

PETER VERKHOVENSKY.
>Who else

SHATOV.
>I don't know

PETER VERKHOVENSKY.
>Listen I'm off to a salon at the Governor's house
>Say hello to your wife for me
>Or is she still in Paris

SHATOV.
>Geneva

PETER VERKHOVENSKY.
>Geneva That's right
>When is she coming back

SHATOV.
>Marie left me four years ago

PETER VERKHOVENSKY.
>That's right I forgot
>You'll have these posters done by tomorrow, won't you

SHATOV.
>I guess

PETER VERKHOVENSKY.
>One more thing:
>This group is my number one priority

If you have any doubts about belonging
I want you to tell me first okay
I don't want to hear it from the others

SHATOV.
I don't have any doubts

PETER VERKHOVENSKY.
I mean it

SHATOV.
I don't have any doubts

PETER VERKHOVENSKY.
See you tomorrow

(Shatov watches him go down the stairs and disappear into the darkness.)

Scene 10

Night. The Governor's salon. Mrs. Lembke, the Governor, Mrs. Stavrogin, and Stepan Verkhovensky applaud Dasha.

STEPAN VERKHOVENSKY.
Brava
Brava

MRS. LEMBKE.
Such a lovely recital
I'm so glad you could come
and entertain us
I know I'm having a wonderful time

MRS. STAVROGIN.
I can tell

STEPAN VERKHOVENSKY.
Isn't she charming
Aren't you a charming hostess

MRS. LEMBKE.
You know something Dorothy
Your daughter looks just exactly exactly like you

MRS. STAVROGIN.
 Dasha's not my daughter

MRS. LEMBKE.
 Yes she is

MRS. STAVROGIN.
 No she's not
 Dasha is my protégé
 Dasha was a serf before the Emancipation
 Tell us about the Emancipation Dasha
 DASHA TELL US ABOUT THE EMANCIPATION
(Dasha hesitates. The hesitation turns into a long, long, long pause.)

DASHA.
 It
(Pause.)

MRS. LEMBKE.
 It must have been very exciting for you

MRS. STAVROGIN.
 It certainly was
 TELL US HOW EXCITING IT WAS DASHA
(Another long pause.)

DASHA.
 It

MRS. LEMBKE.
 Andrei
 I'm going to introduce Dasha to Comrade Turgenev
(To Dasha.)
 Comrade Turgenev is a famous writer you know
 I think he'll want to write about you

STEPAN VERKHOVENSKY.
 Turgenev

MRS. LEMBKE. *(To Stepan Verkhovensky.)*
 Have you heard of Comrade Turgenev

LEMBKE.
 For God's sake Julia
 of course he's heard of Turgenev

>   He's a professor
>   and don't call him Comrade either

MRS. LEMBKE.
>   We've got to use the young people's language Andrei
>   If we don't
>   the young people won't think we're taking them seriously
>   Aren't I right Comrade Verkhovensky
>   It's the only way to avoid a revolution
>
>   Comrade Turgenev is going to be the guest of honor
>   at my charity ball
>   Comrade Turgenev is such a dear friend
>   We've been friends since way back when
>   Someday he's going to write a book about me

STEPAN VERKHOVENSKY.
>   Turgenev God
>   Spare my backside
>
>   Another old goat singing the same old song
>   When was the last time he wrote anything new
>
>   When I was at the University
>   No one paid any attention to Turgenev
>
>   Turgenev was old hat even then
>   and that was twenty years ago
>
>   Nevertheless
>   I'm always amazed the way some people hang on
>
>   with the bourgeoisie
>   Oh the bourgeoisie can never get enough of Turgenev can they
>
>   And I suppose we'll all have to hear from his NNNNOVEL

STAVROGIN.
>   *Guten tag* everyone
>   *(Everyone turns around. Stavrogin is standing in the doorway. His eyes are burning, like two black coals.)*

MRS. STAVROGIN.
>   Nicholas

SHATOV.
   SHIIIIIIIT
(<u>Go To</u>: *Shatov, as he gives the handle of the press an enormous heave, it spits papers and they fly all over the room. Somewhere, two cars crash into each other. Blackout. Lights up: Nicholas Stavrogin is kissing his mother's hand.*)

STAVROGIN.
   Hello mother
   I've been looking for you all over town
(*Everyone stares.*)

LEMBKE.
   So this is the famous Nicholas Stavrogin

MRS. STAVROGIN.
   Governor and Mrs. Lembke
   May I present

MRS. LEMBKE.
   I know who you are
   We've heard all about you
   and that group of anarchists

STAVROGIN.
   What anarchists

MRS. STAVROGIN.
   Don't speak to him
   He'll only contradict you

STAVROGIN.
   No I won't

MRS. LEMBKE.
   Nicholas Stavrogin went to school with Peter
   Peter says Nicholas is his inspiration
   Come sit down beside me Nicholas
   Move Andrei

   Nicholas Stavrogin
   Is it true you stole one of your mother's checks
   and made it out for six hundred marks
   ANDREI MOVE

LEMBKE.
Julia

MRS. LEMBKE.
Nicholas is using the methods of the aristocracy
to support the rise of the proletariat
aren't you Nicholas
I just think it's sooo ironic
though of course one risks alienating one's mother

LEMBKE.
Julia stop it

MRS. LEMBKE.
I'm going to invite you to my charity ball
You and all your friends too
What do you call yourselves
The People's Axe

LEMBKE.
Justice
The People's Justice

STAVROGIN.
I don't think I want to go to any ball

MRS. STAVROGIN.
Nicholas

MRS. LEMBKE.
Nonsense of course you do

STAVROGIN.
And they're not my friends either
I'm not working with them anymore
because it's all defunct isn't it
The Revolution and the Cause etcetera etcetera

LEMBKE.
So
you've stopped working with the anarchists have you

STAVROGIN.
Dead Deader Deadest

MRS. LEMBKE.
>My husband doesn't believe you Nicholas
>He thinks you and all your friends
>are morally corrupt

LEMBKE.
>I do not

MRS. LEMBKE.
>Yes you do Andrei
>For goodness sake you're having them all followed

LEMBKE.
>No I'm not

MRS. LEMBKE.
>Don't look at me like that
>You're having half the town followed
>so look out everybody
>Don't say what you think or my husband will have you followed

LEMBKE.
>That's not funny Julia

STEPAN VERKHOVENSKY.
>He's having me followed
>His snoop even came to my HOUSE

LEMBKE.
>Nobody's following anybody

STEPAN VERKHOVENSKY.
>He knocked on my FRONT DOOR
>He asked me personal questions about my PERSONAL LIFE
>What's his name

LEMBKE.
>Nobody's spying on anybody

MRS. LEMBKE.
>Blum
>His name is Blum

LEMBKE.
>Stop it Julia

STEPAN VERKHOVENSKY.
　I'm going to tell everyone in town
LEMBKE.
　You stop it too old man
　All of you just stop it
STEPAN VERKHOVENSKY.
　In addition to which
　I'm going to write it down in my DIARY
　When I publish my diary
　you'll have to go back to being a
　RAILWAY CLERK
LEMBKE.
　Anarchist
STEPAN VERKHOVENSKY.
　Tyrant
LEMBKE.
　Nihilist
STEPAN VERKHOVENSKY.
　Demagogue
LEMBKE.
　Sex molester
　You're nothing but a sex molester
STEPAN VERKHOVENSKY.
　Libel Libel
LEMBKE.
　You and all your anarchist friends
　They've never gone anywhere or done anything
　They don't even know how to read anymore
　All they know how to do is blow up bridges
STEPAN VERKHOVENSKY.
　WE KNOW EVERYTHING YOU'RE DOING
LEMBKE.
　AND WE KNOW EVERYTHING YOU'RE DOING
STEPAN VERKHOVENSKY.
　WE'VE BEEN WATCHING YOU FOR MONTHS

LEMBKE.
   AND WE'VE BEEN WATCHING YOU FOR MONTHS

STEPAN VERKHOVENSKY.   (Singing.)
   ALLONS ENFANTS DE LA PATRIE
   LE JOUR DE GLOIRE EST ARRIVE

(Stavrogin grabs Stepan Verkhovensky by the lapels, and pulls his head toward him. He pulls him closer and closer, and finally sinks his teeth into the old man's nose. He is hanging on like a bull terrier, as everybody screams.)
   HE'S BITING ME
   HE'S BITING ME

MRS. STAVROGIN.
   I'M GOING TO FAINT

DASHA.
   NICHOLAS

MRS. STAVROGIN, LEMBKE and MRS. LEMBKE.
   STOP THAT
   STOP IT RIGHT NOW
   STOP IT
   STOP IT
   STOPPPPPPITTTTT

(Blum runs up from nowhere, and jumps on Stavrogin's back.)

BLUM.
   I'VE GOT HIM SIR

DASHA.
   GET OFF HIM
   GET OFF HIM

(Dasha tries to pull Blum away from Stavrogin. Under their combined weight, Stavrogin sinks to the floor, his teeth still sunk into Stepan Verkhovensky's nose. Peter Verkhovensky suddenly speaks from the doorway.)

PETER VERKHOVENSKY.
   Good afternoon everybody
   Hello Nicholas Welcome home

MRS. LEMBKE.
   PETER SAVE US

LEMBKE.
> Hello Peter
> As you can see
> we've just had a minor altercation
> but everything's under control now

STAVROGIN. *(To Blum.)*
> Get off

MRS. LEMBKE. *(To Blum.)*
> DON'T GET OFF
> HE'LL MURDER US ALL

LEMBKE.
> I'll handle this Julia
> That's all right Mister Blum
> You can get off him now

(Blum gets off. Stavrogin lies there.)

MRS. STAVROGIN.
> Nicholas you must apologize to Uncle Stepan

MRS. LEMBKE.
> YOU'RE GOING TO BE DEPORTED IF YOU DON'T WATCH OUT

LEMBKE.
> LET ME HANDLE THIS EVERYBODY
> Nicholas
> I know deep down you've got a kind and noble heart
> and obviously you're a man of culture
> but as your friend and Governor

MRS. LEMBKE.
> WE WON'T TAKE YOU SERIOUSLY IF YOU BEHAVE LIKE THIS

LEMBKE.
> Julia I can handle this
> Nicholas
> Why did you bite your uncle Stepan

STAVROGIN.
> I can't tell you

LEMBKE.
Nothing's too awful to tell me Nicholas
STAVROGIN.
God will punish me
LEMBKE.
But I won't
If you come to me with a repentant heart
I will forgive you
(Nicholas looks up at Lembke from the floor. Pause. Finally he speaks.)
STAVROGIN.
All right but I have to whisper
MRS. LEMBKE.
DON'T LET HIM BITE YOU
LEMBKE.
Nicholas won't bite me
will you Nicholas
STAVROGIN.
No of course not
(Slowly, Lembke bends his ear to Stavrogin's lips. Slowly, Stavrogin takes holds of his head, and sinks his teeth into Lembke's ear.)
LEMBKE.
 SHOOT HIM
 SOMEBODY SHOOT HIM
LEMBKE, MRS. LEMBKE, BLUM, and STEPAN. VERKHOVENSKY.
SHOOT HIM SHOOT HIM SHOOT HIM SHOOT HIM
(As Blum, Mrs. Lembke, and Stepan Verkhovensky jump on Stavrogin, <u>Go To</u>: Kirilov writing as fast as he can, in his journal.)
KIRILOV'S VOICE.
 Six o'clock in the afternoon. Outside the temperature is 45 below. Feeling cold and dizzy. Afraid I'll have a fit again tonight. Feels like it. Tongue swollen. Can't do anything. Trying to read.

 Nicholas Stavrogin is back in town. Well so the king is dead. Long live the king.

Scene 11

Morning. Shigalyov's room. Liputin, Shigalyov, and Virginsky are staring at Stepan Verkhovensky, who has a bandage on his nose.

LIPUTIN.
Nicholas Stavrogin is back in town?

STEPAN VERKHOVENSKY.
Yes and he bit me

VIRGINSKY.
Where is he now

STEPAN VERKHOVENSKY.
I wasn't doing anything
I was saying, Nicholas how nice to see you
And I was about to tell him how much we missed him
When he came over to me and bit me

SHIGALYOV.
Where is he now

STEPAN VERKHOVENSKY.
A human-bite is more dangerous than a rat-bite

VIRGINSKY.
He's probably having breakfast with Peter

LIPUTIN.
He's not having breakfast with Peter

SHIGALYOV.
They're probably talking about the strike

VIRGINSKY.
That's why Nicholas Stavrogin has come back
because of the strike

SHIGALYOV.
He's going to climb on top of the bank
and give a speech
like he did the first time

VIRGINSKY.
About what's fair and what's not fair
Them eating caviar while we're starving to death

LIPUTIN.
He's not having breakfast with Peter

VIRGINSKY.
>   How do you know

LIPUTIN.
>   Because I know who Peter is having breakfast with
>   and it's not Nicholas Stavrogin

(Pause.)

SHIGALYOV.
>   Who is it

LIPUTIN.
>   I'm not supposed to tell you

VIRGINSKY.
>   Why not

LIPUTIN.
>   Because it's a secret

(Pause.)

VIRGINSKY.
>   Peter tells you lots of things doesn't he

LIPUTIN.
>   Peter tells me everything

SHIGALYOV.
>   What else does he tell you

LIPUTIN.
>   He told me something really scary
>   but I can't tell you about that either
>   not until it's all over

VIRGINSKY.
>   Not until what's all over

LIPUTIN.
>   I can't tell you

VIRGINSKY.
>   Come on

LIPUTIN.
>   I'll give you a hint
>   Somebody is going to kill himself

VIRGINSKY.
    Who's going to kill himself
LIPUTIN.
    I can't tell you but it's
    somebody we all know
(Suddenly an envelope slips itself under the door. They freeze.)
VIRGINSKY. *(Whispering.)*
    What the hell is that
(Liputin gets up, goes to the envelope, and stands, looking down at it.)
LIPUTIN.
    It's an envelope
VIRGINSKY.
    Don't pick it up
SHIGALYOV.
    Pick it up
(Liputin pushes the envelope with his foot. Nothing. He reaches down, and picks it up. Carefully, he opens it. It's a letter. He reads it aloud.)
LIPUTIN.
    Governor and First Lady Mrs. Lembke
    cordially invite you
    to a Charity Ball
    at the Governor's mansion
    this Friday evening

    Our theme: 'Russia: A New Beginning'
    Our guest of honor: Ivan Sergeyevich Turgenev
    Dinner at ten
    followed by dancing
    Repondez S'il Vous Plait
(Shigalyov takes the invitation, and looks at it.)
SHIGALYOV.
    We've been invited to the Governor's charity ball
STEPAN VERKHOVENSKY.
    I already got my invitation
(Virginsky takes the invitation, and looks at it.)

VIRGINSKY.
> I've lived in this town all my life
> I've worked in this town
> and now I'm starving in this town
> but I've never been invited to the Governor's charity ball

(Peter enters.)

LIPUTIN.
> GOOD MORNING PETER
> TAKE MY CHAIR WHY DON'T YOU

(Everybody shoots to their feet. Peter sets his briefcase on the table.)

PETER VERKHOVENSKY.
> Good morning everyone
> I see you've gotten your invitation
> to the Governor's charity ball
>
> I wouldn't bother responding
> I told them
> to save their charity for themselves

SHIGALYOV.
> Are you going

PETER VERKHOVENSKY.
> Of course not
> and neither is Nicholas Stavrogin
> None of you are going, either
> Where's Shatov

(Pause.)

VIRGINSKY.
> You told them we're not going

PETER VERKHOVENSKY.
> Yes

VIRGINSKY.
> But maybe we'd like to go

PETER VERKHOVENSKY.
> Be sensible Virginsky
> Do you think they're inviting you to their party
> so you can have a good time
> They only want to humiliate you

    in front of their rich friends
    You'll be nothing more than the prize pig at the fair
    Please
    Let's not have anymore talk about it
(Shatov enters. Everybody falls silent, as he goes to the far wall and stands against it, cradling his portfolio.)
    Now that Shatov has arrived
    we can finally get down to business
    Hello Shatov

SHATOV.
    Hello

PETER VERKHOVENSKY.
    Did you bring the posters

SHATOV.
    Yeah

PETER VERKHOVENSKY.
    May we look at them

SHATOV.
    I guess
(Shatov sets his portfolio on the table, takes out a poster, and flattens it on the table. They all lean over, and look at it.)

LIPUTIN.
    What happened

SHATOV.
    I know what you're going to say
    It looks like she's got two heads
    but it's not two heads it's a shadow
    They've both got shadows
(He snatches the poster off the table.)
    If you wanted a good poster
    you should have bought me a better roller
    but we didn't have the money for a better roller did we
    We never have the money for anything
    I'M JUST THE PRINTER

VIRGINSKY.
    You're wrinkling it

SHATOV.
> Fuck it
> I'm not going to be around long enough
> to print anything else
> You want me to get arrested

PETER VERKHOVENSKY.
> Calm down

VIRGINSKY.
> We don't want you to get arrested

SHATOV.
> Fuck you Virginsky

PETER VERKHOVENSKY.
> Excuse me gentlemen
> Excuse me gentlemen

SHATOV. *(To Peter.)*
> YOU THINK I'M STUPID

PETER VERKHOVENSKY.
> When you behave stupidly Yes I do

VIRGINSKY.
> Don't fight everybody
> Don't fight

PETER VERKHOVENSKY. *(To Shatov.)*
> Calm down
> you silly stupid cow

(Shatov spits at Peter. Peter tackles him. As the rest of the gang tries to pull Peter off Shatov, Nicholas Stavrogin enters. Everybody gets up from the floor. Peter wipes the spit off his face.)
> Good morning Nicholas

STAVROGIN.
> Good morning everybody
> I wasn't sure you'd still be meeting in the same place

SHIGALYOV.
> You want to sit down
> You want some vodka

I've got some vodka
but I've only got one glass

LIPUTIN and VIRGINSKY.
Sit down Sit down

STAVROGIN.
No really
I don't want

SHIGALYOV.
He doesn't have to sit down if he doesn't want to

STEPAN VERKHOVENSKY.
You were very good last night by the way
Very convincing
Though you nearly bit my nose off
Still
You made a fool out of the Governor I'll say that

SHIGALYOV.
You look great

VIRGINSKY.
Paris must have been great was it

SHIGALYOV.
Not Paris
Berlin

VIRGINSKY.
Berlin's great too

LIPUTIN.
Let him sit down

STAVROGIN.
I don't want to interrupt your
though obviously I have
so why don't I just get to the
I'll just say what I

GANG.
SPEECH SPEECH

STAVROGIN.
> What I want to say is
> I'm quitting the group
> so now it's official
> as of today
> I'm no longer your leader
> and Peter's your leader
> I've heard what a wonderful job he's been doing for the
>> last year
> two years
> and I'm sure he'll continue doing an even more
>> wonderful job
> especially with your support
> so thank you everybody
> thank you Peter
> If you ever need me

(Stavrogin is backing toward the door. Everybody stares at him. Shatov is the first one to speak.)

SHATOV.
> You're quitting?

STAVROGIN.
> Yes I'm quitting

SHATOV.
> You're going to quit
> Just like that

STAVROGIN.
> Yes

SHATOV.
> Just like that

STAVROGIN.
> Yes

SHATOV.
> I told them you wouldn't quit
> I told them you wouldn't quit
> That's why you didn't write to us Is that it

STAVROGIN.
   Sort of
SHATOV.
   YOU CAN'T QUITTTT
SHIGALYOV.
   Shut up Shatov
SHATOV.
   YOU CAN'T QUITTTT
VIRGINSKY.
   SHATOV
SHATOV.
   I WON'T LET YOU QUIT
   I WON'T LET YOU
   I WON'T LET YOU
(Shatov runs out. Nicholas runs out, too.)
PETER VERKHOVENSKY.
   As you can see Nicholas Stavrogin is upset
   In fact I think he has health problems
VIRGINSKY.
   What kind of health problems does he have
PETER VERKHOVENSKY.
   I don't know Virginsky
STEPAN VERKHOVENSKY.
   Does he have venereal disease
PETER VERKHOVENSKY.
   I don't know Dad
LIPUTIN.
   Does he have smallpox
PETER VERKHOVENSKY.
   I don't think it's any of our business Liputin
   Shall we get on with the meeting
SHIGALYOV.
   I don't see how we can have a meeting
   without Nicholas Stavrogin

VIRGINSKY.
   Maybe one of us should go after him and bring him back

PETER VERKHOVENSKY.
   Gentlemen
   I understand why you're all upset
   Nicholas Stavrogin has always been an important member of this group
   and will continue to be an important influence on our
      mission
   but surely we're not going to let the departure of a single
      individual
   deter us from our course

SHIGALYOV.
   I didn't think he was ever going to come back
   but I didn't think he'd completely quit

VIRGINSKY.
   He's the one who started this group

LIPUTIN.
   What about

PETER VERKHOVENSKY.
   Yes Liputin

LIPUTIN.
   What about Shatov

PETER VERKHOVENSKY.
   I'm sure Shatov will come to his senses
   but let me say this:
   You've been working without Nicholas Stavrogin
   for two and a half years

   When he went to Europe you didn't stop working
   Now that he's quit you won't stop working either
   In fact just now he said
   he wants you to keep working

VIRGINSKY.
   Is that what he said

PETER VERKHOVENSKY.
Yes Virginsky that's exactly what he said

VIRGINSKY. *(To Shigalyov.)*
Is that what he said

PETER VERKHOVENSKY.
Under my official leadership of course
But I don't want to serve as your official leader
unless I have your support
(Pause.)

LIPUTIN.
All those in favor of Peter Verkhovensky
serving as our official leader
raise your hands
(Slowly, they all raise their hands.)
All those against
(They put their hands down.)
All those abstaining
(Silence.)

PETER VERKHOVENSKY.
Thank you Mister Chairman
Thank you gentlemen
Shall we distribute the posters

Scene 12

The sound of the factory, the machinery revving. Shatov runs past Kirilov's door, and scrambles up the stairs to his room. He bursts in, and starts destroying everything. He tears the posters off the wall, he throws his clothes on the floor, he throws his tin dishes on the floor, he throws everything on the floor and stamps on it.

Downstairs, Kirilov's door opens.

KIRILOV.
STOP THAT NOISE
STOP THAT NOISE
STOP IIIIITTTT OR I'LL GET THE POLICE

(Kirilov slams his door shut. Shatov turns to the printing press, which sits on his table. He goes to it, and tries to lift it. It won't budge. He tries again, and this time manages to lift it. He starts to carry it toward the window, but reconsiders. Instead, he staggers out the door. The sound of the factory. Saws grinding. Shatov lugs the printing press down the stairs, flight after flight, pulling it around corners, panting under its weight. As he passes Kirilov's door, Kirilov throws open the door.)

    YOU'RE A PUBLIC MENACE
    THEY'RE GOING TO ARREST YOU FOR BEING A
        PUBLIC MENACE
    IT'S ONLY A MATTER OF TIME
(Kirilov slams the door.)

Scene 13

Day. Lembke's office. Lembke is on his knees, pushing a toy train around a toy village. He has a bandage on his ear. He speaks to the villagers.

LEMBKE.
    My people
    We have come here to dedicate the building
    of a great train station

    The Tsar decided long ago to build this
    great train station
    as a monument
    to his great great

    Something.
    As the Governor
    of this great province
    I will make it my business

    to follow the Tsar's orders
    with the same kind of
    Something
    i.e.

if the Tsar decides
to found a republic in this province
I will consider it my job to found a republic
On the other hand

if the Tsar decides
to blow up a church in this province
I will consider it my job to blow up a church
Ipso facto until the Tsar notifies me of his decision
it will be necessary
for every institution
every church every school and every political group
in this province
to continue to exist
and at the same time continue to
Not exist.
Amen and God bless the Transcontinental Railroad.
(He hits a switch. The train blows up. A trap door opens in the floor. Blum sticks his head into the room.)

BLUM.
Excuse me sir

LEMBKE.
Yes Blum

BLUM.
Peter Verkhovensky just had a meeting with Nicholas Stavrogin
First they had a fight
and then somebody started screaming
and the printer ran out
and then Nicholas Stavrogin ran out after that

I've got a guy following Peter
and another guy following the printer
but the guy following the printer says
there's another guy who lives downstairs
and he's got a gun

LEMBKE.
What kind of gun

BLUM.
    I don't know
    I don't have that many guys

LEMBKE.
Well then you're going to have to get more guys aren't you *(He gets out his wallet, and hands Blum a bill.)*

BLUM.
    Listen sir
    you're new in town
    You want to make friends
    I can understand that

    But when this poster comes out
    it will be too late to make friends
    or do anything else
    Let me arrest Peter Verkhovensky right now

    Today Tonight
    We don't need a reason to arrest him
    Security of the State
    Sedition Who cares

    Do something now before it blows up in your face

LEMBKE.
    Yes of course Right

BLUM.
    Do I have your permission to arrest him

LEMBKE.
    No

BLUM.
    No

LEMBKE.
    Mister Blum I like to think of this province as a beautiful train:
    The Tsar is the engineer of this train
    I am the engine boy

Now the engine boy
never does anything unless the engineer tells him to
You know why

BLUM.
Why

LEMBKE.
Because if he did
the train might go too fast
or go too slow
or run off the tracks altogether
and that would be a disaster, wouldn't it

BLUM.
I guess

LEMBKE.
Therefore
until the engineer says differently
this train
and all the passengers on it
must continue to exist
and continue to Not exist

Now go back to your seat and sit down
(Lembke pushes Blum back down the trap.)

Scene 14

Mrs. Stavrogin's house. Dasha is walking past the front door, wearing a maid's uniform, and carrying a tall pile of linen, as Nicholas Stavrogin runs in, and up the stairs. At the top of the stairs, he jumps into a closet.

DASHA.
Nicholas That's a closet
(She follows him. As she opens the closet, Nicholas drags her inside, as Peter Verkhovensky runs in the front door.)

PETER VERKHOVENSKY.
    NICHOLAS
(The closet door clicks shuts. Peter Verkhovensky goes up the stairs to the closet, and opens it. Nicholas is hiding behind Dasha's skirts.)
    Hello Dasha Don't you look nice today
    Nicholas I'd like to talk to you

DASHA.
    What do you want with him
    Can't you see he's exhausted
(Peter pulls Dasha out of the closet, steps inside, and shuts the door. Dasha stands there, eavesdropping.)

STAVROGIN'S VOICE.
    Look Peter I don't care what you say
    I'm quitting
    I've quit the group and I'm going away
    I haven't come back to do anything but pack

PETER VERKHOVENSKY'S VOICE.
    Yes I understand that Nicholas but
    Fine Fine
    Couldn't you have told me beforehand
    You waltz into an official meeting
    and announce you're quitting
    It makes me look like an idiot

    Nicholas
    Nicholas
    What's the matter with you
(Pause.)

STAVROGIN'S VOICE.
    I want to go to China
    actually

PETER VERKHOVENSKY'S VOICE.
    China

STAVROGIN'S VOICE.
    Canton
    Have you ever been there

PETER VERKHOVENSKY'S VOICE.
   No, and neither have you
STAVROGIN'S VOICE.
   They say it's beautiful
   Mountains
PETER VERKHOVENSKY'S VOICE.
   Yes I know
STAVROGIN'S VOICE.
   Everything is rotten here
   The bottom is falling out
   and the whole thing stinks
MRS. STAVROGIN'S VOICE.   *(From afar.)*
   DASHA.
   DASHA ARE YOU UP THERE
   DASHA WHERE ARE YOU
(Dasha tiptoes downstairs.)
STAVROGIN'S VOICE.
   I know somebody who has a house in Canton
   That's in China
PETER VERKHOVENSKY'S VOICE.
   I know where Canton is
STAVROGIN'S VOICE.
   Have you ever been there
PETER VERKHOVENSKY'S VOICE.
   I already told you
STAVROGIN'S VOICE.
   Right
   Well as far as I'm concerned
   the group belongs to you now
   You can keep running it or you can stop running it
   and go back to Moscow
PETER VERKHOVENSKY'S VOICE.
   Nicholas I don't want to criticize you
   but frankly your timing stinks
   The Society is on the verge of a national strike

STAVROGIN'S VOICE.
> Fuck them
> Fuck the Society
> Fuck them all

PETER VERKHOVENSKY'S VOICE.
> But I don't want to

STAVROGIN'S VOICE.
> That's your decision then
> *(Matryosha comes upstairs, and stops in front of the closet, listening.)*

PETER VERKHOVENSKY'S VOICE.
> Obviously you're having some kind of nervous breakdown

STAVROGIN'S VOICE.
> No I'm not

PETER VERKHOVENSKY'S VOICE.
> Your hands are shaking

STAVROGIN'S VOICE.
> No they're not

PETER VERKHOVENSKY'S VOICE.
> All right fine
> There's going to be a general strike
> and riots maybe
> There are going to be arrests
> and things are going to get really bad
> Now if somebody were to get killed in the middle of it
>
> Nicholas look at me
> Action is what's called for
> Action is what's going to save us
>
> I have this idea about an assassination
> *(Dasha runs up the stairs. She almost knocks on the door, but stops.)*
> I've got somebody who's going to take the blame for it
> but I need to give him 500

STAVROGIN'S VOICE.
> Assassination

PETER VERKHOVENSKY'S VOICE.
> Yes and I need to give him 500

because he's going to write a letter

STAVROGIN'S VOICE.
The group is going to assassinate

PETER VERKHOVENSKY'S VOICE.
Not the group
Me

STAVROGIN'S VOICE.
But the group will be held responsible

PETER VERKHOVENSKY'S VOICE.
Listen Nicholas
you said it's my group now

STAVROGIN'S VOICE.
Yes but
Yes of course

PETER VERKHOVENSKY'S VOICE.
With this act
we will tear ourselves away from the bonds of social order
and social culture
and social laws
and social morals
With this act
we will become the enemy

STAVROGIN'S VOICE.
Yes I
I can see that but I
It's really not what I

PETER VERKHOVENSKY'S VOICE.
NICHOLAS ALL I NEED IS FIVE HUNDRED
(Nicholas Stavrogin jumps out of the closet. Dasha and Matryosha are standing there. Matryosha points to the door, where she has just finished writing the words.)

MATRYOSHA. *(Reading.)*
I
Killed
God
(Stavrogin turns, and hurries off.)

Scene 15

Day. Mrs. Stavrogin's house. The doorbell rings insistently. Dasha appears, carrying buckets.

DASHA.
   WHO IS IT

SHATOV'S VOICE.
   LET ME IN DASHA
   LET ME IN
(She opens the door. Shatov bursts in.)

SHATOV.
   Where's Nicholas

DASHA.
   Ivan go away

SHATOV. *(Calling.)*
   NICHOLAS STAVROGIN I WANT TO TALK TO YOU

DASHA.
   He's not here
   Now get out
   before Mrs. Stavrogin sees you

SHATOV.
   Ow
(She is pushing him out the door, and following him.)
   Nicholas has quit the group, you know

DASHA.
   I know

SHATOV.
   Just like that
   After two and a half years
   Not even a letter
   I wrote him FIVE TIMES

DASHA.
   I'm glad

SHATOV.
> Nicholas doesn't give a shit about us
> and he doesn't give a shit about you either
> You're a fool if you think he's going to marry you
> Do you have any money
> Do you have any money

DASHA.
> No

SHATOV.
> Fuck it
> I'm quitting the group too
> Fuck all of them
> I buried it

DASHA.
> What did you bury

SHATOV.
> Their printing press
> IT WAS A LOUSY PRESS

DASHA.
> You buried the group's printing press

SHATOV.
> If you ask me the whole system is corrupt
> and there's not going to be any revolution
> and we should all give up the idea of equality
> Fuck equality
> The only one who can save us now is God

(She grabs him by the collar, and shoves him up against the wall.)

DASHA.
> It wasn't your press Ivan

SHATOV.
> Yeah well
> Are you going to loan me some money or not

DASHA.
> Where did you bury it

SHATOV.
>　I'm not telling

DASHA.
>　Where did you bury it

SHATOV.
>　In the park
>　By the lake

DASHA.
>　You buried it in broad daylight

SHATOV.
>　Nobody saw me

DASHA.
>　People walk there all the time

SHATOV.
>　Nobody was there

DASHA.
>　It's not enough that you have to hang around those idiots
>　but now you've gone and killed yourself too

SHATOV.
>　I'm not afraid of them

DASHA.
>　They're not the ones you should be afraid of
>　It's the people they work with
>　I told you not to get involved with them, didn't I
>
>　All right fine
>　I'll ask Nicholas to talk to Peter
>　but Ivan you have to go back to the park
>　and dig it up

SHATOV.
>　I don't want Nicholas talking to anyone
>　Nicholas is the one who got me into this mess

DASHA.
>　Where are you going

SHATOV.
> I don't know
> Someplace warm
> Maybe I'll go to Africa or Morocco

DASHA.
> Are you going back to your room

SHATOV.
> Fuck it Dasha
> Let's get out of this place together
> We'll go to Spain and get jobs as gardeners

DASHA.
> No

SHATOV.
> Why not
> It's because you don't want to leave Him, isn't it
> All right
> Give me 200
> and you'll never hear from me again

DASHA.
> Ivan I don't have any money to give you

MRS. STAVROGIN.
> DASHA IS THAT THE COAL MAN

DASHA.
> NO MA'AM

(Dasha pushes Shatov away, and comes back inside to find Mrs. Stavrogin brandishing her checkbook.)

MRS. STAVROGIN.
> I pay that man every month
> but he thinks he can come whenever he wants

DASHA.
> Yes, ma'am

(Mrs. Stavrogin turns and starts heading upstairs.)

MRS. STAVROGIN.
> Never mind
> Let everyone do what they like

I'm just the widow
Widow With a Checkbook

I write out checks to the world
If it's not the coal man or the bread man or the ice man
it's my own son
sitting up there in his room
like the Maharishi
He thinks he can steal my money and then ask for more
but I let him get away with it
because I'm too busy writing checks to the universe
(She turns to Dasha.)
And what about you
You haven't been a bargain to raise either
It costs money to turn a serf
into a socialite

Everybody wants to be a genius
Nobody wants to get a job
(Mrs. Stavrogin disappears into her room and shuts the door.)

Scene 16

Night. The silence is deep and black.

Kirilov is sitting at his table. In front of him is a pistol. He picks it up, and looks at it from every angle. Finally, he points it into his brain. He sits there for some moments, feeling it.

<u>Meanwhile</u>: *Peter Verkhovensky lights a cigarette, sitting at the table. He takes a gun out of his pocket, loads it, and puts it to his head. After a moment, he pulls the trigger — an empty click.*

<u>Go To</u>: *Nicholas Stavrogin hurrying through the dark. Matryosha is following him. She is toying with him — every time he turns and looks back, she freezes. He hurries on, trying to escape.*

<u>Go To</u>: *Shigalyov working quickly, nailing a poster to the factory wall. When he's done, he yells.*

SHIGALYOV.
> TO HELL WITH RUSSIA AND THE WORLD TOO
(He runs away. <u>Go To</u>: Virginsky nailing a poster to a wall. When he finishes, he yells.)

VIRGINSKY.
> DOWN WITH THE TSAR
(He runs away. <u>Go To</u>: Stepan Verkhovensky stuffing a poster into a trash can. He runs away. <u>Go To</u>: Liputin nailing a poster to a door. On the other side of the door, a big dog is barking furiously, straining against his leash. Liputin yells at it.)

LIPUTIN.
> FUCK YOU
(He kicks the door. The dog goes berserk. Liputin runs away.)

Scene 17

Morning. Mrs. Lembke, Mrs. Stavrogin, and Peter Verkhovensky are having breakfast. As Mrs. Lembke holds up the poster, Peter serves tea.

MRS. LEMBKE.
> A jug is useful
> because one may pour water into it
> A pencil is useful because one may write anything with it
> but the Mona Lisa's face
>
> is only a painted face
> and is inferior to anything in Nature
> Crumpet

MRS. STAVROGIN.
> Thank you

MRS. LEMBKE.
> Butter

MRS. STAVROGIN.
> No thank you

MRS. LEMBKE.
>   Take this poster, for example
>   See the woman in this poster
>   This woman is Medusa
>   See the apple in her hand

PETER VERKHOVENSKY.
>   Axe

(Pause.)

MRS. LEMBKE.
>   This axe is only a painted axe
>   Put a real axe beside it
>   Which would you rather have

MRS. STAVROGIN.
>   Personally I think

PETER VERKHOVENSKY.
>   Mrs. Stavrogin would rather have a real axe

MRS. STAVROGIN.
>   Would I

MRS. LEMBKE.
>   Of course you would
>   This is what classical theory boils down to
>   once it is exposed to the light of free investigation
>   Likewise Charity

MRS. STAVROGIN.
>   I never needed a real axe to control you Peter Dear

PETER VERKHOVENSKY.
>   And I won't need a real axe to control you either

MRS. LEMBKE.
>   Aren't we supposed to be planning my party

MRS. STAVROGIN.
>   That's why I'm here

MRS. LEMBKE.
>   Where was I

PETER VERKHOVENSKY.
>   Charity balls

MRS. LEMBKE.
> Most people with their charity balls
> What they like about charity is immoral
> Charity just gives them the chance
> to enjoy their wealth even more.
> In fact:

MRS. STAVROGIN.
> Some children are born angry
> and stay angry the rest of their lives

PETER VERKHOVENSKY.
> Charity corrupts both giver and receiver

MRS. LEMBKE.
> Charity corrupts both giver and receiver
> And besides it only leads to the increase of poverty
> which leads us all to the conclusion
> that charity ought to be forbidden by law
>
> Luckily
> after the revolution
> there will be no poor at all

(Peter Verkhovensky lifts her hand to his lips, and kisses it. The doorbell rings. Mrs. Lembke calls off.)

> MISTER BLUM WOULD YOU GET THE DOOR PLEASE
> MISTER BLUM
> ANSWER THE DOOR BLUM

(No answer. The doorbell rings again. Mrs. Lembke gets up, and goes out to answer it. <u>Go To</u>: the other side of the wall. Lembke and Blum are eavesdropping.)

LEMBKE.
> Spouting Fourier
> She thinks Mrs. Stavrogin will be impressed

(Into the listening device.)
> I'M NOT IMPRESSED EITHER

BLUM.
> Well it's too late now
> That poster is hanging all over town
> The steel factory is nearly out of control
> Twelve workers have been fired

    We nearly had a riot on our hands
    Three people went to the hospital

    and the man who started it
    is sitting right here in your parlor
    making love to your wife

LEMBKE.
    All right all right

BLUM.
    Do something right now
    Arrest him

LEMBKE.
    All I wanted
    was to be governor of a quiet little province
    I wanted a quiet little province where nothing ever happens

BLUM.
    You're the leader
    You're the representative of the Tsar
    the most powerful leader in the entire world

LEMBKE.
    But what if we arrest him and he doesn't confess
    We'll have to let him go
    I'll be a laughing-stock
    The whole town will laugh at me

BLUM.
    This town would never dare laugh at you
    This town is terrified of you

LEMBKE.
    It is?

BLUM.
    Put Peter Verkhovensky in jail
    and your face will be on the cover of
    every civil service magazine
    in the country

(Mrs. Lembke knocks on Lembke's door.)

MRS. LEMBKE.
ANDREI THERE'S SOMEONE OUT HERE TO SEE YOU
(Lembke goes to the door. Blum gets there first.)

BLUM.
Ask who it is

LEMBKE.
Who is it

MRS. LEMBKE.
IT'S A POLICEMAN
ANDREI WHAT ARE YOU DOING IN THERE

BLUM. *(Low, to Lembke.)*
Give me your permission to arrest Peter Verkhovensky

LEMBKE.
I can't

BLUM.
Give me your permission to arrest Peter Verkhovensky

MRS. LEMBKE.
ANDREIIIII
ANDREEIIII
OPEN THIS DOOR
(She is pushing on the door. Blum pushes back.)

BLUM.
Give me your permission to arrest Peter Verkhovensky

LEMBKE.
All right Do what you want
but oh God
if you screw it up
(Blum jumps down the trap, as Mrs. Lembke pushes the door open.)

MRS. LEMBKE.
It's Lieutenant Somebody
He wants to talk to you about the steel factory
(Lembke is climbing under the desk.)

LEMBKE.
   TELL HIM I'M BUSY
   TELL HIM I'M OUT
   AND I DON'T KNOW WHEN I'LL BE BACK

Scene 18

Night. Dasha is getting ready for bed, when her window opens. Grunting, heaving, and coughing like an old dog, Nicholas Stavrogin hauls himself into view. He is trying to climb into the room, and has only succeeded in wedging himself into the window-frame, when she speaks.

DASHA.
   What are you doing
STAVROGIN.
   Shhhhh Shhhh Shhhh
   I'm trying to
(He yanks his foot into the room, and then manages to follow with the rest of his body.)
DASHA.
   Why didn't you just walk up the stairs
STAVROGIN.
   Don't wake up my mother
(He goes to her. She pushes him away.)
DASHA.
   She wouldn't have heard you
STAVROGIN.
   I want
   All I want
   I just want to hold you
DASHA.
   You could have broken your neck
STAVROGIN.
   Okay Okay Listen

    I'm going to
    shit
    I'm going to China next week
    Canton actually
    Do you want to come with me

DASHA.
    China

STAVROGIN.
    They've got mountains
    I know this place where we could stay
    It's very peaceful

DASHA.
    Don't do that
(He is undressing her.)

STAVROGIN.
    I just want to

DASHA.
    MRS. STAVROGIN

STAVROGIN.
    Shhh

DASHA.
    MRS. STAVROGIN

STAVROGIN.
    I want you to come to China with me

DASHA.
    Why would I want to go to China with you
(He is kissing her.)
    You never once wrote me
    You promised to write but you didn't
    My brother wrote to you five times
    but you never answered him either
    and I don't like the way you bite people
    I think it's strange for a man to bite people
    especially a man like you
    a man everyone respects
    or at least that's what they say

(She is kissing him back.)

STAVROGIN.
>God
>Compared to me
>compared to me
>you're sane
>Really and and and wise and good
>You really are a good person
>You are
>but I'm getting out of this
>this whole country
>This whole country is
>I'm going to China
>I'm going to China
>and grow my hair into a long braid
>down the middle of my back
>Please
>let's not talk anymore
>Lie down

DASHA.
>I have to talk to you about Ivan

STAVROGIN.
>Lie down and let me

DASHA.
>Ivan's in trouble

STAVROGIN.
>I just want to

DASHA.
>You're the only one who can talk to Peter

STAVROGIN.
>I just want to hmmmm

DASHA.
>Nicholas

(He is starting to cry, crumbling before her eyes.)

STAVROGIN.
>I've done something terrible

> I've done something really terrible
> something really horrible
> Mmmmmmmmm soft thighs
> Soft little feet

DASHA.
> Nicholas what's the matter

STAVROGIN.
> I'm going to have to pay for it
> I know I'm going to have to pay for it
> God is going to punish me
> He's going to find me out and punish me
> Wherever I go Wherever I go
> He'll find me

> Hide me
> Hide me

(He pushes his way into her bed, finding her body with his hands, desperate. They begin to make love. Outside, the sound of the factory, churning and grinding, getting louder and louder. Suddenly, people are pounding on Mrs. Stavrogin's front door.)

BLUM, THIRD DEPT. OFFICER 1 and 2'S VOICES.
> OPEN UP
> OPEN UP
> OPEN UP

BLUM'S VOICE.
> KICK IT IN

(Dasha jumps out of bed and runs to the door.)

DASHA.
> WHO'S THERE

BLUM'S VOICE.
> KICK IT IN

DASHA.
> MRS. STAVROGIN

THIRD DEPT. OFFICER 1'S VOICE.
> I'M NOT GOING TO KICK IT IN
> YOU KICK IT IN

(The sound of running, doors slamming.)

MRS. STAVROGIN.
   DASHA

DASHA.
   GOD HELP US

BLUM'S VOICE.
   OPEN UP OR WE'LL BREAK IT DOWN

DASHA.
   WHO'S OUT THERE

THIRD DEPT. OFFICER 1'S VOICE.
   KICK IT IN ASSHOLE

BLUM, THIRD DEPT. OFFICER 1 and 2'S VOICES.
   KICK IT IN
   KICK IT IN

(Blum and two men break in. They wear black leather coats and their heads are covered with black leather masks. <u>In Dasha's room</u>: Peter Verkhovensky arrives, climbing in Dasha's window.)

PETER VERKHOVENSKY.
   Come on

STAVROGIN.
   What are you doing here

PETER VERKHOVENSKY.
   Come on

(Peter drags Nicholas out the window, as Blum and his men ransack the house.)

BLUM.
   WHERE IS HE
   WHERE IS HE

DASHA.
   WHERE'S WHO
   I DON'T KNOW WHO YOU'RE

BLUM.
   BITCH

(Officer 1 pushes Dasha to the floor. Officer 2 runs up the stairs, past Mrs. Stavrogin, who clings to the banister in her nightgown.)

MRS. STAVROGIN.
  WHO ARE YOU LOOKING FOR
DASHA.
  RUN
BLUM.
  PETER VERKHOVENSKY
  WHERE IS PETER VERKHOVENSKY
(Officer 2 opens the closet, and pulls out Stepan Verkhovensky.)
STEPAN VERKHOVENSKY.
  DON'T HURT ME
  PLEASE DON'T HURT ME
BLUM.
  BRING HIM DOWN HERE
MRS. STAVROGIN.
  STEPAN
STEPAN VERKHOVENSKY. *(Turning, pointing at Mrs. Stavrogin.)*
  I DIDN'T DO IT
  SHE MADE ME DO IT
  IT WAS ALL HER FAULT
MRS. STAVROGIN.
  WHAT DID I DO
BLUM. *(To Stepan Verkhovensky.)*
  WHERE IS YOUR SON
MRS. STAVROGIN.
  I DIDN'T DO ANYTHING
BLUM. *(To Stepan Verkhovensky.)*
  WHERE IS YOUR SON
STEPAN VERKHOVENSKY.
  WHO
(Officer 2 pushes Stepan Verkhovensky down the stairs. Mrs. Stavrogin and Dasha scream.)
DASHA.
  NOOOO
(Blum crosses to Stepan Verkhovensky, and kneels on his chest.)

BLUM.
> TELL ME WHERE YOUR SON IS
> OR I'LL ARREST YOU AND EVERYBODY IN THIS HOUSE

STEPAN VERKHOVENSKY.
> I DON'T KNOW WHAT YOU'RE

DASHA.
> DON'T KILL HIM

(Officer 1 kicks Dasha.)

MRS. STAVROGIN.
> DON'T YOU TOUCH HER
> DON'T YOU TOUCH HER

(Officer 2 slugs Mrs. Stavrogin in the face.)

BLUM.   *(To Stepan Verkhovensky.)*
> WHERE'S YOUR SON
> WHERE'S YOUR SON

STEPAN VERKHOVENSKY.
> HE'S NOT HERE

BLUM.   *(To Stepan Verkhovensky.)*
> WHERE'S YOUR SON
> WHERE'S YOUR SON

(He stands up. Officer 2 comes over, and kicks Stepan Verkhovensky in the stomach. As Dasha lunges to help Stepan.)

DASHA.
> NOOOO

(Officer 1 kicks Dasha again. The sound of furniture turning over, glass breaking, shelf after shelf of books falling on the floor. <u>Meanwhile:</u> Kirilov is writing in his room.)

KIRILOV.
> God tells us that life is pain and fear. He also tells us that we must love life, and so we do. But this is a lie, and it's how God keeps us in our chains.

(Blum watches Officers 1 and 2 beat up Stepan Verkhovensky.)

BLUM.
> WHERE'S YOUR SON
> WHERE'S YOUR SON

STEPAN VERKHOVENSKY.
He's not here
(Officer 2 kicks Stepan in the stomach, and Officer 1 kicks him in the back, as Kirilov continues.)

KIRILOV.
Here is the truth: those of you who are afraid to die will always be slaves. For you, there will never be anything but pain and fear.

BLUM.
WHERE'S YOUR SON
WHERE'S YOUR SON
(Stepan coughs, and coughs.)
Jesus
You're not going to throw up are you
(They wait until Stepan Verkhovensky stops coughing.)
Kick him again
(As they start kicking him again: <u>Go To:</u> Nicholas Stavrogin running into the dark. <u>Go To:</u> Peter Verkhovensky running into the dark. <u>Back To:</u> Kirilov, writing in his journal.)

KIRILOV.
But those of you are not afraid to die: if you are brave enough to kill yourself, you will kill your fear. And if you kill your fear, you will kill Him, He who is a fake god, He who is nothing but a slave-master.
And that will be the revolution.
Everybody in the world will be transformed. All minds and all hearts. Even the earth and the universe will be transformed. And history itself will be divided into two parts: the part before we murdered God, and the part after.

END OF ACT ONE

ACT TWO

Scene 1

Day. Shatov is asleep in bed. Someone is pounding on the front door.

MARIE SHATOV'S VOICE.
  SHATOV
  SHATOV
  SHATOV
  SHATOVVVVV
(Shatov opens his eyes.)

SHATOV.
  Who is it

MARIE'S VOICE.
  ALL RIGHT FINE DON'T LET ME IN
  BUT DON'T BE A COWARD JUST SAY IT
  SAY YOU'RE NOT GOING TO LET ME IN
(Shatov sits bolt upright in bed.)
  IVAN SHATOV YOU'RE AN ASS AND AN IDIOT

SHATOV.
  MARIE IS THAT YOU

MARIE'S VOICE.
  OPEN THE DOOR
  OPEN THE DOOR
(Shatov throws open the door to his room, and yells over the railing.)

SHATOV.
  MARIE IS THAT REALLY YOU MARIE

MARIE'S VOICE.
  IVAAANNNNN

SHATOV.
  WAIT
  WAIT I'M COMING
  I'M COMING
  DON'T GO AWAY

(He runs down the stairs, stumbles, pushes himself to his feet, and throws open the door. It's Marie Shatov, looking enormous. As she shoves her bag at him.)

    Marie

MARIE.
    It's me all right
    Don't touch me
    I couldn't stand it if you touched me

SHATOV.
    What are you doing here

MARIE.
    I've only come for a few days
    that's all
    I want you to put me up while I look for work
(She suddenly sits down, and has a coughing fit.)

SHATOV.
    Marie
(She stops coughing, and starts climbing the stairs ahead of him.)

MARIE.
    God I'm tired tired tired
    I took a train
    Eighteen hours from Geneva to Prague
    Took another train as far as the border
    Crossed the border on foot
    I was so afraid someone would recognize me
    I wouldn't have come back except I'm broke
    What a rotten town and it stinks too
    Now I remember why I left
    I left because I had to get a breath of fresh air
(She falls on the stairs, coughing.)

SHATOV.
    Marie are you all right

MARIE.
    Yes it's becoming a really good-looking town
    now that you've burned down half of it

SHATOV.
> Yes Isn't it awful
> People keep setting it on fire

MARIE.
> Is it you and that group of yours

SHATOV.
> No

MARIE.
> Are you still preaching at them

SHATOV.
> I don't preach at them

MARIE.
> I knew you'd never stop preaching
> Once I thought you were going to drive me completely around the bend

(Shatov opens his door, and she goes in.)
> It used to be bad
> but it wasn't this bad

SHATOV.
> You should see it when it snows
> May I take your suitcase

MARIE.
> You did already

SHATOV.
> I mean your coat
> I can take your coatsssss
> Goodness you're wearing a lot of coats

MARIE.
> I'm cold

SHATOV.
> Well then
> It's good you've got them

(She sinks onto the bed.)

MARIE.
> All I want is a glass of tea

SHATOV.
> Stay here
> Don't move
> I'll be right back

(She starts coughing again, as he stumbles down the stairs, winging his way around corners and plunging to Kirilov's door, pushing it open. Kirilov is lifting weights. He looks up.)
> Kirilov
> Guess what Do you have any tea
> Guess what My wife has come back to me

KIRILOV.
> YOU'RE NOT ALLOWED IN HERE

SHATOV.
> Yes I know and I'm sorry but I
> My wife My wife has come back to me
> Isn't it wonderful
> Don't you think it's wonderful
> but if you could only see how tired she is
> I've just got to give her something

KIRILOV.
> Why

SHATOV.
> Because
> Because she's come a long way
> All the way from Geneva

KIRILOV.
> No I mean
> Why did she come back to you

SHATOV.
> Why

KIRILOV.
> Forget it
> It's not important

Of course your wife must have tea
and she must have bread
and
and take some cheese too

but this is for her
understand
I'm doing this for her
not you
You're not allowed to eat any of this

SHATOV.
Thank you Kirilov
Thank you Thank you Thank you

KIRILOV.
DON'T TALK TO ME
YOU'RE NOT ALLOWED TO TALK TO ME

SHATOV.
You know, Kirilov
Deep down you're a very generous man

KIRILOV.
GET OUT
(Shatov runs up the stairs with the tray of food. When he gets to the door of his apartment, he stops. Marie is fast asleep on the bed. From this angle, it's suddenly obvious; she's hugely pregnant. Shatov nearly drops the tray. After a moment, he puts it down, and sneaks up to her, quietly, full of wonder, putting his hand on her belly. Suddenly Peter Verkhovensky appears on the stairs.)

PETER VERKHOVENSKY.
Have you got a woman in there

SHATOV.
What are you doing here

PETER VERKHOVENSKY.
Who is she
(Shatov goes out, keeping Peter in the hallway.)

SHATOV.
Fuck you

> Don't talk to me
> I'm quitting that's what
> I'm quitting you and your
> All of you The whole group

PETER VERKHOVENSKY.
> I see

SHATOV.
> Shut up
> You and Nicholas Stavrogin too
> You're both a couple of
> elitists

PETER VERKHOVENSKY.
> Elitists

SHATOV.
> I mean Nihilists
> So what Go to hell
> I hope you both get arrested

PETER VERKHOVENSKY.
> Listen I'm sorry about the scene the other day
> If you want to quit
> of course you must

SHATOV.
> Just like that
> You're letting me quit Just like that

PETER VERKHOVENSKY.
> I don't want to let you quit but
>
> I talked to Nicholas Stavrogin
> and he agrees with me
> You're not going to contribute much to the group
> in your condition
>
> Don't worry
> He was angry
> and I had to do a bit of fast talking on your part
> but I think he's all right about it now

SHATOV.
>	What has he got to be angry about
>	He's the one who let us down

PETER VERKHOVENSKY.
>	Just hand over the printing press
>	and that will be the end of it

SHATOV.
>	I don't have the press anymore

(Pause.)

PETER VERKHOVENSKY.
>	What did you do with it

SHATOV.
>	I got rid of it

(Pause.)

PETER VERKHOVENSKY.
>	Frankly Shatov
>	You were given a lot of responsibility
>	when you were given that press

SHATOV.
>	I buried it

(Pause.)

PETER VERKHOVENSKY.
>	That was an odd thing to do
>	Where did you bury it

SHATOV.
>	I'm not telling

PETER VERKHOVENSKY.
>	You're not going to tell me

SHATOV.
>	Not until I'm safe
>	I'm getting out
>	I'm going to Africa
>	After I get there I'll write you a letter
>	and tell you where it is

PETER VERKHOVENSKY.
> Surely you realize
> you won't be safe until
> until you give the press back

SHATOV.
> I'm not afraid of you

PETER VERKHOVENSKY.
> And I'm not afraid of you either

(Peter starts to leave. Shatov lunges after him.)

SHATOV.
> I'll go to the Third Department
> I will
> I'll tell them all about you and the Society too

PETER VERKHOVENSKY.
> Good day

(Peter goes. Shatov runs back into his room, locks the door. Marie is awake.)

MARIE.
> You coward
> You're not going to tell the Third Department about anybody
> God why did I come back here
> Why didn't I stay in Switzerland

SHATOV.
> DON'T BOTHER ME I'M TRYING TO THINK

(As Peter passes Kirilov's door, Kirilov opens it.)

KIRILOV.
> Have you got my 500 yet

(Peter hurries away.)

Scene 2

Morning. Lembke and Blum in the Governor's office.

LEMBKE.
> You weren't supposed to arrest Stepan Verkhovensky
> You were supposed to arrest PETER Verkhovensky

BLUM.
   Yes I know

LEMBKE.
   Stepan Verkhovensky is the father
   Peter Verkhovensky is the son

BLUM.
   Yes I know

LEMBKE.
   So why did you arrest the father

BLUM.
   Because

LEMBKE.
   Because why

BLUM.
   Because I couldn't find the son

LEMBKE.
   Don't whine Mister Blum
   The next person who whines
   is going to get slugged in the face

BLUM.
   I'm sorry sir
(Lembke slugs him in the face.)

LEMBKE.
   I'M GOING TO BE THE LAUGHING-STOCK OF
   THIS ENTIRE COUNTRY

Scene 3

Morning. Shigalyov's room. Shigalyov, Virginsky, Liputin, and Peter Verkhovensky enter. Peter is carrying his briefcase.

SHIGALYOV.
   I don't think we should be meeting here
   I think it's dangerous to meet here

VIRGINSKY.
> That guy has been watching this building all morning

PETER VERKHOVENSKY.
> Don't worry
> If he was going to arrest you
> he'd have done it already

LIPUTIN.
> Peter's right
> I saw somebody watching my house this morning
> He could have arrested me but he didn't

PETER VERKHOVENSKY.
> My father was arrested last night

SHIGALYOV.
> What did you say

PETER VERKHOVENSKY.
> My father was arrested last night
> The Third Department broke into his house
> They took all his papers and beat him up
> They beat up everybody else in the house too
> Luckily Nicholas Stavrogin managed to get out

SHIGALYOV.
> FUCK FUCK FUCK FUCK

LIPUTIN.
> Shut up Shigalyov

PETER VERKHOVENSKY.
> Shigalyov I think it's time for you to calm down

SHIGALYOV.
> I DON'T WANT TO CALM DOWN

PETER VERKHOVENSKY.
> All right then don't calm down

(Pause.)

SHIGALYOV.
> So why did they arrest your father
> and not the rest of us

PETER VERKHOVENSKY.
  I don't know
SHIGALYOV.
  YOU'RE LYING
PETER VERKHOVENSKY.
  Excuse me Shigalyov
SHIGALYOV.
  WHY DON'T YOU WANT US TO GO TO THE PARTY
PETER VERKHOVENSKY.
  The party
SHIGALYOV.
  The Governor's party
  I want to know
  why you don't want us to go to the Governor's party
PETER VERKHOVENSKY.
  I don't care if you want to go to the Governor's party
  but as I said before
  it's going to be full of socialites
  and I don't think you'll have any fun
SHIGALYOV.
  THAT'S NOT WHY
PETER VERKHOVENSKY.
  Why do you think I don't want you to go
SHIGALYOV.
  I don't know why
  Because you've got a plan of some kind
  that's why
  and I want to know what your plan is
PETER VERKHOVENSKY.
  You're not making sense Shigalyov
SHIGALYOV.
  I WANT TO KNOW WHAT YOUR PLAN IS
  I WANT TO KNOW WHAT YOUR PLAN IS
  AND I WANT TO KNOW WHO'S GOING TO KILL
    HIMSELF TOO

(Pause.)

PETER VERKHOVENSKY.
   Excuse me

LIPUTIN.
   I didn't tell them anything

SHIGALYOV.
   HE TOLD US EVERYTHING
   AND I WANT TO KNOW WHO IT IS

PETER VERKHOVENSKY.
   I can't tell you that Shigalyov
   What would happen if you were arrested
   I'm not just thinking of your own security
   I'm thinking of the security of every man in this group

SHIGALYOV.
   Oh really

PETER VERKHOVENSKY.
   Yes really

SHIGALYOV.
   Are we the only group you're working with

PETER VERKHOVENSKY.
   Are you what

SHIGALYOV.
   ARE WE THE ONLY GROUP YOU'RE WORKING WITH
   ARE YOU WORKING WITH ANOTHER GROUP
      BESIDES US

PETER VERKHOVENSKY.
   Mister Chairman
   this meeting seems to have gone off-track

SHIGALYOV.
   DON'T GIVE HIM THE FLOOR
   VIRGINSKY AND I HAVE THE FLOOR

LIPUTIN
   Maybe we could all take turns having the floor

SHIGALYOV.
> WE'VE GOT THE FLOOR AND WE'RE NOT GIVING
>   IT UP

PETER VERKHOVENSKY.
> All I'm trying to do is get the meeting back on-track

SHIGALYOV.
> I think Peter's going to do something at the ball
> and I think this person killing himself is part of it
> and I think Peter is working with another group
> and that's the reason he doesn't want us to go to the
>   party
> am I right
> am I right

PETER VERKHOVENSKY.
> Are you

SHIGALYOV.
> How should I know
> Everything's a secret with you
> I don't even know where you live

LIPUTIN.
> I know where he lives

PETER VERKHOVENSKY.
> Nobody knows where I live
> Not even my father knows where I live
> and that's the way I want it

SHIGALYOV.
> Well I think that's strange
> I think that's pretty fucking weird and strange
> You've been our leader for two years now
> and if you expect us to trust you

PETER VERKHOVENSKY.
> Are you saying you don't trust me Shigalyov

SHIGALYOV.
> No
> Shit yes

PETER VERKHOVENSKY.
　　You don't trust me
SHIGALYOV.
　　Virginsky doesn't trust you either
VIRGINSKY.
　　It's not that I don't trust you exactly
SHIGALYOV.
　　IF WE'RE GOING TO BE A GROUP WE CAN'T HAVE
　　　　ANY MORE SECRETS
PETER VERKHOVENSKY.
　　All right no more secrets
　　I've been trying to protect you
　　and so far I've been succeeding
　　because the Governor's wife likes me

　　I always tell her you're just a bunch of guys
　　who get together to argue about politics and play cards
　　Now if you'd like her to think something else
　　that's fine too

　　but it means she'll tell her husband
　　and it means you'll be more likely to get arrested
LIPUTIN.　*(To Shigalyov.)*
　　Now he's mad see
　　See what you're making him do
PETER VERKHOVENSKY.
　　I'm not mad Liputin
　　If the members of this group would like to be
　　publicly identified
　　I applaud their bravery
VIRGINSKY.
　　Maybe we should table this discussion for now
　　and get back to the strike
LIPUTIN.
　　I agree
(Shigalyov is silent.)

PETER VERKHOVENSKY.
>   Don't worry Shigalyov
>   I have a plan for Governor Lembke
>   but right now we have a more important problem:
>   Ivan Shatov has quit the group

(Pause.)

VIRGINSKY.
>   He's quit

SHIGALYOV.
>   Shatov

LIPUTIN.
>   I suppose it's all because of Nicholas Stavrogin

PETER VERKHOVENSKY.
>   You might say so
>   but it's a bit more complicated than that
>   Actually he's buried our printing press

(Another pause.)

VIRGINSKY.
>   Oh come on

SHIGALYOV.
>   That little idiot

LIPUTIN.
>   Why did he do that

PETER VERKHOVENSKY.
>   Because he wants money to get out of the country

LIPUTIN.
>   Money

PETER VERKHOVENSKY.
>   If we don't pay him to dig it back up
>   he says he'll go to the Third Department

VIRGINSKY.
>   But that's
>   that's blackmail isn't it

LIPUTIN.
>   I'm not going to pay him anything

SHIGALYOV.
> FIRST THERE WAS THE GOVERNOR'S PARTY
> AND THEN THERE WAS SOMEBODY KILLING
> > HIMSELF
> AND NOW THERE'S SHATOV

LIPUTIN.
> SHIGALYOV SHUT UP

(To Peter.)
> What do you suggest we do

PETER VERKHOVENSKY.
> I'm not sure
> Shatov has been our friend for years now
> He's upset about Nicholas Stavrogin of course
> and we've all known for years
> that he's more loyal to Nicholas Stavrogin
> than he is to all of you

VIRGINSKY.
> But what do you think we should do

PETER VERKHOVENSKY.
> I can't tell you what to do
> You'll have to think of a solution yourselves
> You're all adults
> You've started a strike
> You're obviously capable of even more radical action

SHIGALYOV.
> We just have to tell Shatov to stop being an asshole

VIRGINSKY.
> But he's blackmailing us

LIPUTIN.
> What if he goes to the Third Department

PETER VERKHOVENSKY.
> You don't have to decide what to do right now
> Shatov will probably give you a little more time
> but I'd like to say one more thing:
>
> There's a point in the life of any group
> when a certain crossroad is reached

and when a certain crossroad is reached
one characteristic becomes more important than any other
and that is the characteristic of loyalty

VIRGINSKY.
We're loyal

SHIGALYOV.
CRAP

LIPUTIN.
ORDER

SHIGALYOV.
I'm not going to let some overgrown student
who's never worked for a living
accuse me of not being loyal to this group

LIPUTIN.
ORDER ORDER ORDER

PETER VERKHOVENSKY.
Mister Chairman may I continue

LIPUTIN.
You may continue

PETER VERKHOVENSKY.
I think it's time for us all to take a loyalty oath
I think we should each
swear loyalty to the Society
and to the group as a whole
the two of them together not separate

VIRGINSKY.
Oh God oh God oh God oh God oh God

PETER VERKHOVENSKY.   *(To Virginsky.)*
Swear

VIRGINSKY.
I swear

PETER VERKHOVENSKY.   *(To Liputin.)*
Swear

LIPUTIN.
I swear

PETER VERKHOVENSKY. *(To Shigalyov.)*
   Swear

SHIGALYOV.
   I hate loyalty oaths

LIPUTIN and VIRGINSKY.
   Shigalyov

SHIGALYOV.
   I swear

Scene 4

Mrs. Stavrogin's house. Mrs. Stavrogin is covering her black eye with makeup, while Stepan Verkhovensky holds a poultice to his eye.

Elsewhere: Nicholas Stavrogin sits on Dasha's bed, writing. Dasha enters.

DASHA.
   Nicholas have you talked to Peter yet
   Nicholas have you talked to Peter yet
(He shakes his head, and keeps writing.)
   Ivan's all by himself over there
   He hasn't got anyone to protect him
   and if Peter gets mad at him because of the press
   Or if the Third Department finds out
   he was the one who printed the posters
   STOP WRITING
(She snatches the pen out of his hand.)

STAVROGIN.
   It's too late

DASHA.
   Your mother got out of bed a few minutes ago
   You should see what her face looks like
   She's never been punched in the face before
   Nicholas

   Nicholas I have an idea
   I think you should go to the Governor and tell him what

happened here last night
Tell him the Third Department was here
and they beat us all up

STAVROGIN.
Why

DASHA.
Because he's the Governor
He ought to know what the Third Department did to us

STAVROGIN.
The Governor already knows
what the Third Department did to you
He's the one who ordered it

DASHA.
He's not the one who ordered it
How could
Why would the Governor order the Third Department
to beat us up
We sat in his salon three days ago
We had tea with him and his wife
He even invited us to his party

STAVROGIN.
But that's how it works you see

DASHA.
That's not how it works

STAVROGIN.
He's the fisherman
and we're the fish
He always puts a nice fat juicy worm on his hook
because he knows the fish will always eat it

DASHA.
Does he expect us to come to his party tonight
even after he's had us beaten up

STAVROGIN.
Yes
You and my mother will go to his party
You'll put on your best party clothes

and you'll smile your prettiest smiles
You'll both have a marvelous time
and at the end of the evening
you'll both forgive him for everything he's done to you

My mother will forgive him
because she likes eating those nice fat juicy worms
but you'll forgive him
because it's what Jesus would have done

DASHA.
No I won't
I won't

STAVROGIN.
Yes you will
and that's what separates you from the rest of the fish
Dasha Shatov

DASHA.
I won't

STAVROGIN.
Listen to me
This is my confession
I'm writing down my confession right here
It's going to be pages and pages
When I'm done I'm going to give it to you

DASHA.
What confession
What are you confessing

STAVROGIN.
Not yet
I have to finish writing it

DASHA.
But you haven't done anything worth confessing

STAVROGIN.
See
You don't know what I've done
but you're already forgiving me

>   Dasha I want you to promise
>   that you'll mail these pages to all the newspapers
>   I want it published in every major newspaper in the
>   country
>   and Europe too
>   It really ought to be published in Europe

DASHA.
>   Why don't you want to mail it yourself

STAVROGIN.
>   Because I'm going to China

(He tries to get away from her, but she catches him, and holds onto him.)

DASHA.
>   You're not really going to China

STAVROGIN.
>   Yes I am

DASHA.
>   Stop saying that

(He tries to get out the door. She slams it, and stands in his way.)

STAVROGIN.
>   Dasha do you believe in ghosts

DASHA.
>   You can't scare me by talking about ghosts either

STAVROGIN.
>   Yesterday
>   a ghost came up to me
>   and said he needed money
>   to commit a murder
>
>   He needs five hundred
>   to commit a murder
>   and I don't even know who it is
>   What scares me is
>   I don't even care who it is
>
>   And though it's vile and it's disgraceful
>   and I should be shocked

>   I can't get it out of my head
>   *I could actually have someone killed*
>   Should I do it Dasha
>
>   At this moment
>   I'm completely conscious of my
>   of the evil in me
>   and it feels somehow
>
>   actually I'm ecstatic
>   I've never felt this good in my life
>   I feel as if I'm standing at the barrier
>   waiting for my enemy to fire
>
>   Should I do it Dasha

DASHA.
>   You're not evil

STAVROGIN.
>   Yes I am
>   I have the evil in me
>   And now you do too

DASHA.
>   No

STAVROGIN.
>   Even the saints
>   Even Jesus
>   Jesus had the evil in him

DASHA.
>   It's not true what you're saying about Jesus and them
>   but I'll say one thing
>   if you made a deal with that ghost
>   you'd better go find him
>   and take it back

STAVROGIN.
>   I can't

DASHA.
>   You'd better
>   You'd better go find him

and take it back

STAVROGIN.
But I don't want to

DASHA.
YOU HAVE TO

STAVROGIN.
What if he wants to murder you

It's the demon
It's the demon in my head
and he's a nasty little demon
with a cold in his nose

a nasty sniffling scabby little demon
and he keeps saying:
Give him the money
Give him the money

(She grabs him.)

DASHA.
Don't say that

STAVROGIN.
What if he wants to murder my mother
What if he wants to murder your brother
What if he wants to murder a little girl
because he wants to murder something
because he wants to take it out on something
that won't fight back

DASHA.
No

(He is struggling to free himself.)

STAVROGIN.
RUN
RUN
RRRRRUNNNNN

(He frees himself from her, and runs away.)

Scene 5

Day. Mrs. Stavrogin is putting another poultice on Stepan Verkhovensky's face.

STEPAN VERKHOVENSKY.
   GENTLY
   GENTLY
MRS. STAVROGIN.
   I'm being as gentle as I can
STEPAN VERKHOVENSKY.
   This isn't going to work
   This never works
   IT HAS TO BE VINEGAR
(He throws the poultice on the floor.)
   They punched me
   and they kicked me
   And they took all my papers
   and my manuscript too
   I WORKED ON THAT MANUSCRIPT FOR EIGHT YEARS
MRS. STAVROGIN.
   You can start over
STEPAN VERKHOVENSKY.
   The greatest collection
   of Spanish Literature ever
   The entire Golden Age under a single cover
   I'm going to sue them that's what
   I'M GOING TO SUE THEM
(He bursts out crying, and hits his pillow with his fist. She hands him a handkerchief. He blows his nose.)
   And then you know what else happened
   You know what else
MRS. STAVROGIN.
   What

STEPAN VERKHOVENSKY.
> I was lying on the floor
> when I opened my eyes and saw the lieutenant
> I saw the lieutenant standing over me
>
> and suddenly I nearly
> I nearly grabbed his ankle
> and bit it

MRS. STAVROGIN.
> You what

STEPAN VERKHOVENSKY.
> An officer of the Third Department
> I nearly bit an officer of the Third Department
> A man with a gun in his hand

(He starts crying again.)

MRS. STAVROGIN.
> Stop it Stop it
> You've been hoping to get arrested for 15 years
> Well now you've finally done it
> You've gotten yourself arrested
> and nearly gotten us both killed
> Where are you going

STEPAN VERKHOVENSKY.
> I'M GOING TO THE GOVERNOR'S BALL
> I'M GOING TO CONFRONT THE GOVERNOR IN
>   FRONT OF THE WHOLE TOWN
> IN FRONT OF TURGENEV TOO
> I'M GOING TO MAKE HIM GIVE MY BOOKS BACK
> IF IT'S THE LAST THING I DO
> I WAS A PROFESSOR AT ST. PETERSBURG

MRS. STAVROGIN.
> DON'T YOU DARE MAKE A SCENE AT THE
>   GOVERNOR'S PARTY

STEPAN VERKHOVENSKY.
> I'LL SHOW YOU
> I'LL SHOW ALL OF YOU

MRS. STAVROGIN.
>   IF YOU MAKE A SCENE AT THE GOVERNOR'S PARTY
>   I'LL CUT YOU DEAD
>   COME BACK HERE
>   I'M NOT GOING TO LET YOU MAKE A FOOL OF ME
>   STEPAN VERKHOVENSKY

(He runs out, then runs back in.)

STEPAN VERKHOVENSKY.
>   DAVID AND GOLIATH
>   THAT'S WHAT THIS IS
>   I'M DAVID AND I'M GOING OUT TO FIGHT GOLIATH

MRS. STAVROGIN.
>   COME BACK HERE

(He runs out.)

STEPAN VERKHOVENSKY'S VOICE.
>   I JUST HOPE I DON'T BITE ANYBODY

Scene 6

Day. Kirilov's room. Kirilov is slumped at the table, his gun in his hand. A knock. Peter enters.

PETER VERKHOVENSKY.
>   KIRILOV

(Pause. Kirilov opens his eyes.)

KIRILOV.
>   What are you doing here

PETER VERKHOVENSKY.
>   Are you all right

KIRILOV.
>   I'm fine

(Kirilov gets up, and starts pouring himself a cup of tea.)

PETER VERKHOVENSKY.
>   You know Kirilov

>   I envy you
>   living here in your quiet little room
>
>   free to explore the life of the mind
>   while I run around and around
>   like a mouse in a cage
>
>   I must have talked to 20 people today
>   and it's not even 2 o'clock in the afternoon
>   Are you sure you're not sick

KIRILOV.
>   What do you want

(Pause.)

PETER VERKHOVENSKY.
>   The Governor is throwing a big party tonight
>   and I'm going to kill him

KIRILOV.
>   Tonight

PETER VERKHOVENSKY.
>   Yes

KIRILOV.
>   What about my 500

PETER VERKHOVENSKY.
>   I have to be honest with you Kirilov
>   I'm having problems getting your 500
>   Frankly I don't think I can do it

KIRILOV.
>   That's not my problem

PETER VERKHOVENSKY.
>   I know it's not your problem
>   but I'm just wondering if

KIRILOV.
>   If you don't have the money
>   I won't write the letter

PETER VERKHOVENSKY.
>   Listen Kirilov
>   You don't have any reason to be mad at me

I'm not the one who sent you to America
and I didn't abandon you there, either

KIRILOV.
Get out

PETER VERKHOVENSKY.
Not yet

KIRILOV.
Get out
(Peter picks up Kirilov's gun, and looks at it. Kirilov takes the gun from Peter.)
You might kill Governor Lembke tonight
but tomorrow morning absolutely nothing will have changed
You'll still be afraid of God
and you'll still be afraid of dying
(Peter walks out.)

Scene 7

Shigalyov's room. Virginsky bursts in.

VIRGINSKY.
I've been trying to get into your building for two hours
That guy is still out there
did you see him

SHIGALYOV.
Shut the door

VIRGINSKY.
Shit he's a big guy
and he's got his hands in his pockets
I'm not scared
I'm glad we did it
I feel like I could take on the whole government

But on the other hand
I went into the bathroom this morning
I wasn't gone two minutes

When I came back somebody had searched my room
Whoever it was he drank my cup of coffee
That takes a lot of nerve, don't you think

What's that
(Shigalyov is pouring a canister of liquid into a small flask.)

SHIGALYOV.
Hand me that rag
(Virginsky picks up the rag, and hands it to Shigalyov, who pushes it into the flask, and seals it, as:)

VIRGINSKY.
What are you doing

SHIGALYOV.
I'm thinking about what I'm going to wear
to the Governor's party

VIRGINSKY.
The Governor's party

SHIGALYOV.
Don't you want to go to the Governor's party

VIRGINSKY.
Sure but Peter doesn't want us to go

SHIGALYOV.
I think I'm going to go as
Honest Russian Thought

VIRGINSKY.
What's Honest Russian Thought

SHIGALYOV.
Exactly
It's been centuries since anyone in this country
has had an honest Russian thought
They've all been too busy
wearing French clothes
and German haircuts
and listening to Italian opera

VIRGINSKY.
Yeah but

SHIGALYOV.
　Yeah but what
(Virginsky watches Shigalyov pick up another bottle, and start pouring kerosene into it.)

VIRGINSKY.
　You're building a bomb
(Shigalyov lights a match.)

SHIGALYOV.
　How fast can you run

Scene 8

Evening. Lembke follows Mrs. Lembke around, as she gets dressed for the party.

MRS. LEMBKE.
　TWO HUNDRED PEOPLE
　I'VE GOT TWO HUNDRED PEOPLE COMING IN TWO HOURS
　HOW AM I GOING TO HOLD UP MY HEAD
　WHAT AM I GOING TO SAY TO THEM
　TWO HUNDRED PEOPLE

　LAST NIGHT MY HUSBAND ARRESTED ONE OF THE MOST INTELLIGENT MEN IN THIS PROVINCE
　HE'S A PROFESSOR
　HE SPEAKS FRENCH
　YOU KNOW HOW MANY PROFESSORS WE HAVE IN THIS TOWN
　ONE
　AND MY HUSBAND ARRESTED HIM

LEMBKE.
　They were supposed to arrest Peter Verkhovensky

MRS. LEMBKE.
　DON'T TALK TO ME
　I CAN'T STAND IT WHEN YOU TALK TO ME

(Suddenly a sneeze erupts from behind the door. Mrs. Lembke goes to it, and opens it. Blum is standing there.)

What did you say Mister Blum

BLUM.

I didn't say anything ma'am

MRS. LEMBKE.

Well Mister Blum YOU'RE FIRED

(She slams the door. Then she sits down, and starts putting on her stockings.)

Peter Verkhovensky is not only a genius
He's in love with me and worships the ground I stand on
He's the leader of his entire generation
If you arrest him you'll have a revolution on your hands
Don't do that

(Lembke has pulled the second stocking away from her. He's biting and tearing at it, like a wild animal.)

LEMBKE.

I'm doing it
I'm doing it

MRS. LEMBKE.

Give it to me

(She grabs it back. It is torn.)

LEMBKE.

That's what you get
That's what you get
for talking to me in that tone of voice
You and your female mannerisms
This is no salon
This is the GOVERNOR'S MANSION

I am the GOVERNOR OF THIS PROVINCE
and I am
and I am
caught in a balloon
a balloon

MRS. LEMBKE.

What for God's sake are you talking about

LEMBKE.
>I could SHOULD
>have been able to cope with this job
>I've got the ability
>I can do this job I can
>
>But my life has consisted of you
>and people like you
>telling me every hour of every day
>that I'm a fool
>that I don't exist
>that I'm a villain
>
>So I spend all my waking hours
>proving to everyone that I'm not a fool
>and I'm not a villain
>and yes I do exist
>and I'll arrest who I want
>when I want

MRS. LEMBKE.
>Are you challenging me

LEMBKE.
>Challenge Madame
>If Peter Verkhovensky comes to this house tonight
>I'll have him arrested
>
>I don't need a reason to arrest him
>Conspiracy, that's what
>and I won't have him in this house ever again
>
>Oh God I've done it now

MRS. LEMBKE.
>Jealous
>You're jealous of Peter Verkhovensky

LEMBKE.
>Jealous
>Everybody in this town is laughing at me
>and you're the one who put them up to it

MRS. LEMBKE.
>That's right I did it all
>I'm responsible for the mess you're in
>The mess you created by arresting the wrong man

LEMBKE.
>You will not talk to me like that
>You won't You won't
>I'll cancel your party
>I'll tell them all not to come
>I can do that

MRS. LEMBKE.
>Just try it

LEMBKE.
>I'll arrest them
>I'll arrest everyone who comes to this party
>It's YOUR friends who are responsible for all this
>They're the ones who have been writing those
>anonymous letters and printing those posters
>I know who they are and I know where they live too

MRS. LEMBKE.
>Look at you
>You're getting completely carried away

LEMBKE.
>CARRIED AWAY
>IT'S TOO LATE TO GET CARRIED AWAY
>WE'RE ON THE BRINK OF A REVOLUTION
>AND IT'S ALL MY FAULT

MRS. LEMBKE.
>Nonsense

LEMBKE.
>Don't say Nonsense
>You can't say Nonsense to me
>I'll arrest you
>I'll arrest you
>and that lover of yours

MRS. LEMBKE.
　HA

LEMBKE.
　I WILL

MRS. LEMBKE.
　HA
　　HA
　　　HA

LEMBKE.
　JULIA

(He raises his fist to strike her. She raises a hand to protect herself. But he doesn't strike her. He turns and rushes away: the sound of a flock of birds, taking flight.)

Scene 9

Night. Stavrogin is feverish and shaking. He struggles to keep writing, but his hand keeps jumping off the page.

Matryosha crouches in the corner, endlessly wrapping and unwrapping her jump-rope around her neck.

Peter enters.

PETER VERKHOVENSKY.
　Nicholas I've come to a decision

　Remember what you said about China
　Well I'm beginning to think it's a good idea
　In fact maybe we should go together

　You're the only one who really understands me
　and I'm the only one who really understands you
　What do you think

STAVROGIN.
　Please don't

PETER VERKHOVENSKY.
    You said it yourself
    Everything here is rotten

    And the Society
    The Society's changed
    All they ever talk about now
    is obedience
    Fuck obedience
    Let's go to China together
    We'll start all over again

STAVROGIN.
    I don't think I want to start all over again

PETER VERKHOVENSKY.
    But if it were the two of us

STAVROGIN.
    That's
    No that's ridiculous

PETER VERKHOVENSKY.
    Well that's honest
    Never mind I understand perfect
    Actually I haven't been sleeping well at
    My mind is

    My mind seems to be
    It's all because of Ivan Shatov
    I'm really upset about him Nicholas
    You were the one who brought him into the group

    I'll never know what you saw in him
    and now he's buried the group's printing press
    He's buried the press
    and he's not going to give it back

    I mean Christ
    You can't bring somebody like that
    into a group like this
    Someone who thinks freedom means getting away from
        the farm

Someone who has no understanding of the context
Never mind Never mind
Meanwhile the group thinks I'm the one
who's trying to get them arrested ME

I told them I'm the one who's kept them from being arrested
but everything I said
seemed to excite them even more
Finally I made them take a loyalty oath

but that might have been the wrong thing to do too
Nicholas
Nicholas if you don't mind my asking
Why don't you want me to go to China with you
(No response.)
You're not worth it
You're not worth throwing my life away
I got into this mess because of you

Ever since that night at the University
I was studying for my orals remember
when you came into my room with a bottle of vodka

You sat in my room for three hours
talking about the meaning of Democracy
and what we should do together after the Revolution

You made my ears ring you really did
And when you said let's climb up to the roof of the library
we actually did

We climbed up to the roof of the library

Only when we got up there
we were too drunk to climb down
so we sat there together

watching the sunrise
and it sounds truly corny now
but I remember thinking:

I'm watching the dawn of a new civilization
This is the Greeks
This is the Romans

This is the dawn of an entirely new civilization
and I'm sitting here with Nicholas Stavrogin
watching it

STAVROGIN.
Yes I remember

PETER VERKHOVENSKY.
No you don't

Listen
I'm going to assassinate the Governor tonight
and I need my 500

STAVROGIN.
Um

PETER VERKHOVENSKY.
Did you ask your mother

STAVROGIN.
No

PETER VERKHOVENSKY.
Of course I can see why you'd be hesitant to ask your mother
considering how much she hates me
But I need that 500 to go forward Nicholas

STAVROGIN.
I don't
I don't want to assassinate anyone

PETER VERKHOVENSKY.
You're not going assassinate him Nicholas
I'm going to assassinate him
but I need the money now

God look at me
I'm standing in an aristocrat's dressing room

begging for money
This is a truly pathetic moment in my life
I NEED THAT MONEY NOW NICHOLAS STAVROGIN.
I'm sorry
(Peter rushes up to Stavrogin, and feints a blow to Stavrogin's head. Stavrogin ducks.)

PETER VERKHOVENSKY.
I'm leaving now
If I get arrested tonight
you'll only have yourself to blame
(Peter goes out.)

Scene 10

Night. Peter Verkhovensky on "How to Kill a Philosopher."

PETER VERKHOVENSKY.
How to kill a philosopher:

Hemlock
Conium maculatum
a member of the carrot family

Umbelliferae
Strip its leaves and boil the stem
until you've got a nice hot tea

Poor Socrates
Not a very dignified way to die
He drank it all the way down

and then he began to walk around the room
and eventually he began to feel
a queer sort of heaviness in his legs

so he lay down on his back
and when the guard came in
the guard put his hand on Socrates' feet and said

Can you feel this
No, said Socrates
Then the guard put his hand on Socrates' legs and said

Can you feel this
No, said Socrates
Socrates was possessed all over

by a kind of numbness
Then the numbness became a shaking
and the shaking became an earthquake

and the earthquake became a tidal wave
Blood was erupting from every hole
By the time the guard put his hand on Socrates' heart

Socrates was staring up at the cold stone ceiling
mistaking it for the sky
which was the end of western philosophy

and the beginning of justice

Scene 11

Night. The Governor's salon. The room is dimly lit.

Upstairs, an enormous party is in progress. Lights are burning. Shadows flare against the wall, and a hundred pairs of feet can be heard, pounding to a ferocious polka.

Downstairs, Shigalyov enters from the dark, followed by Virginsky.

VIRGINSKY.
　Shigalyov wait a minute
SHIGALYOV.
　Hear that
　It's a polka
　When was the last time you heard a polka

When was the last time
you got some pretty girl drunk
and made her dance to a polka

VIRGINSKY.
Stop
Don't run like that
If you trip you'll explode

SHIGALYOV.
I hope I explode
I want to explode

(As Shigalyov heads toward the staircase, the music stops. Laughter. Gloved applause. The sound of glasses, clinking. Murmuring. Liputin appears at the top of the stairs, coming down. He is dressed to the nines, and carrying an empty plate.)

LIPUTIN.
I've been looking for you guys
Why didn't you come in the main entrance

VIRGINSKY.
Don't ask me
Ask Shigalyov

LIPUTIN.
Shigalyov
Christ what's the matter with you
You look like a convict

SHIGALYOV.
I'm an Honest Russian Thought

LIPUTIN.
What's that

SHIGALYOV.
Exactly
Do you know how long it's been
since anyone in this country
had an honest Russian thought

VIRGINSKY.
Liputin he's got a bomb
in his coat

Show him the bomb Shigalyov
Show it to him
(Shigalyov takes the loaded flask out of his coat. Liputin pushes it back.)

LIPUTIN.
For Christ's sake
What are you doing
There are 200 people up there
Get out of here
Get out

SHIGALYOV.
Make me

LIPUTIN.
Virginsky get him out of here

SHIGALYOV.
Peter thinks we're just a bunch of back-water farm-boys
Let's show him what back-water farm-boys can do

VIRGINSKY.
Shut up
(The men pull back into darkness, as Mrs. Lembke appears at the top of the stairs, accompanied by Blum, who's carrying a bottle of champagne. As Mrs. Lembke and Blum descend:)

MRS. LEMBKE.
I don't understand where everyone is
Where are the people from the high school
and the convent
and the Post Office
Didn't they get their invitations

BLUM.
It's not my job to deliver invitations

MRS. LEMBKE.
What about the people from the steel factory

BLUM.
They're in jail

MRS. LEMBKE.
> They were supposed to be let out of jail
> so they could come to my ball

BLUM.
> They're criminals

MRS. LEMBKE.
> Then what about the people from the Teachers Guild
> and the Secretaries Guild
> and the Blacksmiths Guild
> and the Weavers Guild
> HOW CAN WE HAVE A NEW BEGINNING IN THIS
>   COUNTRY
> IF NOBODY CAN BE BOTHERED TO SHOW UP

BLUM.
> If you want my opinion

(She slaps him. He reels.)

MRS. LEMBKE.
> Tell the Governor I slapped you
> Go on I dare you

(Blum and Mrs. Lembke stop, as they suddenly see Shigalyov, Virginsky, and Liputin standing in the dark.)
> Well hello everybody
> What are you doing down here in the dark

BLUM.
> These are Peter Verkhovensky's friends

VIRGINSKY.
> We're looking for Peter

MRS. LEMBKE.
> Peter's upstairs

BLUM.
> Go on
> Get upstairs

SHIGALYOV.
> Don't talk to us like that
> We're guests

VIRGINSKY.
   Don't touch me

SHIGALYOV.
   Don't touch him
   Let go of him

MRS. LEMBKE.
   Mister Blum
   Stop it
   Stop it
   Stop it
(Blum lets go of Virginsky's coat.)
   So you're Peter's friends
   Peter tells me so much about you
   Why I feel as if I already know you
(To Shigalyov.)
   Which one are you
(Pause.)

SHIGALYOV.
   Shigalyov

MRS. LEMBKE.
   Shigalyov isn't that a nice earthy name
   Would you like to dance with me Mister Shigalyov

SHIGALYOV.
   Down here

MRS. LEMBKE.
   No upstairs
   when the music starts
   Mister Blum
   take the champagne to the kitchen
   and open it
   We'll give Peter's friends a glass of champagne

VIRGINSKY.
   Can I have something to eat

MRS. LEMBKE.
   I'm sorry Mister What's your name

SHIGALYOV.
    Virginsky

MRS. LEMBKE.
    Virginsky but we don't have anything to eat
    because this afternoon the chef decided to go on strike
    him and his two knock-kneed assistants
    They've all gone on strike isn't that wonderful

      I said I've got 200 people coming any minute
      but if you people need to go on strike
      then that's exactly what you should do
      because we'll do anything it takes to avoid a revolution
      Open the champagne Mister Blum
(Blum goes off to the kitchen, carrying the champagne.)
    Peter doesn't understand
    I ordered 200 bottles of champagne for this party
    but he always likes to bring his own
    So how long have you been playing cards
(Pause.)

VIRGINSKY.
    Five years

LIPUTIN.
    Four

MRS. LEMBKE.
    Isn't that nice
    My husband used to have a card game
    every Saturday afternoon
    It was absolutely relentless
(Dasha and Mrs. Stavrogin appear at the top of the stairs, coming down.)

DASHA.
    Mrs. Lembke may I speak to you and your husband

MRS. STAVROGIN.
    Good evening Mrs. Lembke what a fabulous party

MRS. LEMBKE.
    Good evening Mrs. Stavrogin
    Good evening Dasha
    What lovely gowns

DASHA.
>I'd like to speak to you now if I may

MRS. LEMBKE.
>I'm sorry Dasha
>The Governor's not here
>Maybe he's with the people from the Miners' Guild
>and the Carpenters' Guild
>and the Whatnot Guild
>Where are they Mister Blum

(Blum is arriving from the dark, carrying the open champagne bottle.)

BLUM.
>I wouldn't know ma'am

MRS. LEMBKE.
>You're a spy aren't you
>It's your job to know where everyone is
>OH LOOK HERE COMES MY HUSBAND

(Lembke climbs in the window. His clothes are covered with mud, he has grass in his hair, and he's wearing a necklace of daisies around his neck. Mrs. Lembke takes a stiff sip from her champagne glass, and crosses to him. Mrs. Stavrogin gives Dasha a pinch.)

DASHA.
>OW

MRS. STAVROGIN.
>How dare you speak to the Governor's wife like that
>This is a party
>not a political meeting

(Blum gets to Lembke first.)

BLUM.
>Where have you been
>Everyone on your staff has gone on strike except me

MRS. LEMBKE.
>Andrei where have you been
>We've been waiting for you all night

>What in God's name are these
>Daisies

(Shigalyov goes up to Lembke.)

138

SHIGALYOV.
>   Guess what I am

BLUM. *(Intervening.)*
>   Get out of here

SHIGALYOV.
>   I'm an Honest Russian Thought
>   Do you know what an Honest Russian Thought is

(Blum pulls Lembke toward the stairs.)

BLUM.
>   Listen sir I'm getting very nervous
>   I'm getting very very nervous here

MRS. LEMBKE.
>   Nonsense
>   These people are Peter's friends

BLUM.
>   Yes but if they attack
>   it will be the three of us against the three of them

(Stepan Verkhovensky appears at the top of the stairs, coming down.)

STEPAN VERKHOVENSKY.
>   May I say Madame Lembke
>   You are looking
>   simply charmante this evening

MRS. STAVROGIN. *(Interrupting.)*
>   Oh that's hilarious coming from you
>   If you say one word about your books
>   I'll tell them to throw you out

(Lembke suddenly wrenches himself free from Blum, and turns to face the gang, Stepan Verkhovensky, Mrs. Stavrogin, and Dasha.)

LEMBKE.
>   Good citizens

MRS. LEMBKE.
>   Andrei

LEMBKE.
>   GOOD CITIZENS
>   WELCOME TO THE GOVERNOR'S MANSION

TO THE BALL
TO THE BALL
(Pause.)

MRS. LEMBKE.
    Andrei what are you talking about
    All right say it
    Finish it whatever you're going to say
(A long pause.)

LEMBKE.
       IT

MRS. LEMBKE.
    Don't say "it"
    Say something Anything

LEMBKE.
       IT
(A burst of big, phony laughter comes out of mid-air.)
    What was that
    Did you hear that

MRS. LEMBKE.
    Hear what
    I didn't hear anything
    Keep talking

LEMBKE.
    Somebody was laughing at me
    WHO WAS LAUGHING AT ME

MRS. LEMBKE.
    Andrei get a grip on yourself
(Another burst of big, phony laughter.)

LEMBKE.
    THE NEXT PERSON WHO LAUGHS WILL BE
        UNDER ARREST

VIRGINSKY.
    I didn't hear anyone laughing

MRS. LEMBKE.
    Ladies and gentlemen

> The Governor is so glad you were able to come
> and now he wants to invite you all upstairs
> to dance

(As Mrs. Lembke starts dragging her husband up the stairs.)

STEPAN VERKHOVENSKY.
> Excuse me Governor but before you go
> I'd like to speak to you about my books

LEMBKE.
> You're him
> You're the one who was laughing
> Arrest this man

STEPAN VERKHOVENSKY.
> I want my books back

MRS. LEMBKE.
> We don't know what happened to your books old man

MRS. STAVROGIN.
> Stepan Verkhovensky get away from there

BLUM.
> Come on old man
> You're under arrest

STEPAN VERKHOVENSKY.   *(To Blum.)*
> Don't you touch me
> Don't you touch me
> Don't you come near me

SHIGALYOV.
> Don't push him you asshole

(As Blum starts slapping handcuffs on Stepan Verkhovensky, the music erupts again — a ferocious combination of drum, accordion, and horn. Shigalyov, Liputin, and Virginsky try to intervene.)

STEPAN VERKHOVENSKY.
> I AM PROFESSOR STEPAN VERKHOVENSKY
> I AM A SCHOLAR AND A WRITER
> AND I WANT MY BOOKS BACK

MRS. LEMBKE.
> ALL RIGHT ALL RIGHT YOU'LL GET YOUR BOOKS
> BACK

    WE'LL HAVE THEM SENT TO YOUR HOUSE

SHIGALYOV and LIPUTIN.
    LET GO OF HIM

MRS. STAVROGIN.
    OH GOD HE'S GETTING ARRESTED AGAIN

STEPAN VERKHOVENSKY.   *(To Lembke.)*
    I WANT TO SAY SOMETHING HERE
    YOU MAY BE THE GOVERNOR
    BUT IF YOU THINK YOU CAN GO AROUND
        ARRESTING PEOPLE
    AND BEATING THEM UP

MRS. STAVROGIN.   *(To Blum.)*
    LET GO OF HIM

(Mrs. Stavrogin tries to hit Blum, but accidentally hits Virginsky, instead.)

VIRGINSKY.
    OW

STEPAN VERKHOVENSKY.
    IT'S A LOT EASIER TO ARREST SOMEBODY AND
        BEAT THEM UP
    THAN IT IS TO HAVE AN IDEA

LIPUTIN.
    YOU TELL HIM GRANNY

SHIGALYOV.
    IT'S A LOT EASIER TO KILL SOMEBODY TOO

MRS. LEMBKE.
    ANDREI HURRY UP

DASHA.
    EVERYBODY STOP PUSHING

STEPAN VERKHOVENSKY.
    CERVANTES

(Everyone is on the stairs, now — a knot of people struggling with each other.)

BLUM.
>   THE NEXT PERSON WHO TOUCHES ME IS UNDER ARREST

STEPAN VERKHOVENSKY.
>   LOPE DE VEGA

DASHA.
>   STOP PUSHING EVERYBODY

STEPAN VERKHOVENSKY.
>   CALDERON DE LA BARCA

MRS. LEMBKE.
>   ANDREI

STEPAN VERKHOVENSKY.
>   THE GOLDEN AGE WAS WORTH MORE THAN ANY OF YOUR
>   STUPID CHARITY BALLS
>   AND MORE THAN YOUR EMANCIPATION PROCLAMATION
>   AND EVEN MORE THAN THE REVOLUTION

LIPUTIN.
>   WHAT ABOUT SHAKESPEARE

STEPAN VERKHOVENSKY.
>   I'D GIVE THE ENTIRE REVOLUTION
>   FOR A SINGLE SONNET BY SHAKESPEARE
>   BECAUSE I CAN LIVE WITHOUT BREAD
>   BUT I CANNOT LIVE WITHOUT BEAUTY

BLUM.
>   OWWWWWWWWWW

(Stepan Verkhovensky has sunk his teeth into Blum's hand. Blum socks him in the face, and he falls down the stairs.)

MRS. STAVROGIN.
>   STEPAN

DASHA.
>   MISTER VERKHOVENSKY

BLUM.
>THAT SON OF A BITCH BIT ME

SHIGALYOV.
>GO ON GRANNY
>BITE HIM AGAIN AND I'LL SET THE WHOLE PLACE ON FIRE

BLUM.
>I'LL BITE ANYONE WHO BITES ME

LIPUTIN.
>BITE THE GOVERNOR GRANNY
>GO ON AND BITE HIM

(The gang pursues the Lembkes and Blum up the stairs. Shigalyov struggles to get the flask out of his pocket. The music gets louder.)

LIPUTIN, VIRGINSKY, and SHIGALYOV.
>BITE THE GOVERNOR
>BITE THE GOVERNOR

LEMBKE.
>YOU'RE ALL UNDER ARREST
>EVERYBODY IS UNDER ARREST

MRS. LEMBKE.
>HELP
>MISTER BLUM HELP US

BLUM.
>LET'S GO BACK TO THE PARTY GOVERNOR

LIPUTIN, VIRGINSKY, SHIGALYOV, and STEPAN VERKHOVENSKY. *(Continuing.)*
>BITE THE GOVERNOR
>BITE THE GOVERNOR
>BITE THE GOVERNOR

DASHA.
>LET'S ALL GET OUT OF HERE

MRS. STAVROGIN.
>STEPAN VERKHOVENSKY COME WITH US

LIPUTIN, VIRGINSKY, SHIGALYOV, and STEPAN
VERKHOVENSKY.
    BITE THE GOVERNOR
    BITE THE GOVERNOR
DASHA.
    MRS. STAVROGIN LET'S GET OUT OF HERE
BLUM.
    LET'S GO NOW GOVERNOR
    LET'S GO NOW GOVERNOR
(Liputin, Shigalyov, Virginsky, and Stepan Verkhovensky are closing in on the Governor as:)
LEMBKE.
    I'LL BITE YOU BACK
    I'LL BITE YOU BACK
DASHA.
    EVERYBODY LOOK
    EVERYBODY LOOK
LIPUTIN, VIRGINSKY, and SHIGALYOV.
    BITE THE GOVERNOR
    BITE THE GOVERNOR
DASHA.
    LOOK EVERYBODY LOOK
(Everybody stops.)
    SHE'S BLEEDING
(Upstairs, the music stops. A smattering of applause, laughter. Mrs. Lembke is sputtering blood. Blood is coming out of her mouth, and nose. She tries to keep climbing the stairs, falls down.)
MRS. LEMBKE.
    Thank you everyone
    I've had a wonderful evening
    but now I'm afraid
    Peter
(Mrs. Lembke collapses.)
LEMBKE.
    Julia
    Julia get up This isn't funny

DASHA.
> She's sick

LEMBKE.
> Julia

BLUM.
> The drink

(As Blum takes the champagne glass out of her hand, a big burst of phony laughter explodes.)

DASHA.
> GET A DOCTOR
> SOMEBODY GET A DOCTOR

BLUM.
> YOU'RE UNDER ARREST
> NO ONE IS ALLOWED TO LEAVE THIS ROOM
> YOU'RE ALL UNDER ARREST

DASHA.
> GET A DOCTOR

LEMBKE.
> JULIA

(Shigalyov, Virginsky, Liputin, Mrs. Stavrogin, Stepan Verkhovensky, and Dasha flee. Peter Verkhovensky appears at the top of the stairs, sees what's happening, and runs away. <u>Go To:</u> Shatov's room. Marie is lying on the bed, moaning, and coughing. Shatov sits beside her, wiping the sweat off her face. <u>Go To:</u> Nicholas Stavrogin running, Matryosha chasing him. <u>Go To:</u> Kirilov writing frantically in his journal.)

KIRILOV'S VOICE.
> 3 A.M. A light rain has begun to fall. I heard the library was on fire. I went to watch it burn. A mob of people, talking about an assassination. Some of them crying. All of them half-dead from the smoke. The firemen screaming at us to move. Why did we stand there, staring into the blaze? What's so irresistible about watching your own city burn?

END OF ACT TWO

ACT THREE

Scene 1

Dawn. Dasha's room. Far-off: the distant clang of firebells. The sound of rain, drumming on the roof. Nicholas Stavrogin is asleep on Dasha's bed, spattered with mud, still wearing his boots, his papers sticking out of his coat. Dasha sleeps in a nearby chair.

In the corner, Matryosha skips rope:

MATRYOSHA.
In a forest deep and icky
Lived a cockroach whose name was Nicky.
One day Nicky up and dived
Into a glass of hungry flies.

Said the flies to Mister Nicky,
"You can't come in here wicky-wicky
We're cannibals and we'll eat you up.
We'll make you into cockroach soup."

Nicky got scared and he tried to get out,
But the top was too high and the walls were too stout.
So in the end our little friend
Was eaten up from end to end.

(Nicholas wakes up, crying out. Dasha wakes up. <u>Go To:</u> Shatov's room, as Marie wakes up, crying out, clutching her belly in pain. Shatov wakes up on the floor. <u>Back To:</u> Dasha's room, as Peter Verkhovensky climbs in the window.)

PETER VERKHOVENSKY.
    Nicholas

STAVROGIN.
    Get away from me

DASHA. *(To Peter.)*
    What are you doing here

PETER VERKHOVENSKY.
>I've got to talk to Nicholas

DASHA.
>No

PETER VERKHOVENSKY.
>I'VE GOT TO TALK TO NICHOLAS

(Peter pushes Dasha out the door, and locks it behind her.)
>Dasha must have told you
>we had a bit of a debacle last night
>The Governor's wife ended up
>dead

(Stavrogin buries his head under his pillow. Peter pulls the pillow off Stavrogin's head. Stavrogin covers his ears with his hands. Peter pulls Stavrogin's hands away from his ears, as:)
>Smell that That's the garbage dump
>Somebody set it on fire last night
>There's a crowd of people running around with axes too
>and Nicholas you'll appreciate this

>The drivers are on strike
>I couldn't even get a carriage to come here
>I had to walk
>Isn't that brilliant

>Yes the whole night was brilliant
>Killing the Governor's wife
>Killing someone who wasn't even political
>Eureka

>Maybe the less political they are the better
>Maybe it's the method that makes it political
>not the person
>what do you think Nicholas

STAVROGIN.
>Ah Yes That's a wonderful idea

PETER VERKHOVENSKY.
>This is my strike
>I'm the one who started it
>Nobody wanted to print those posters

They were too scared to do it

but I forced them to do it
and now look what's happened Even you
you didn't think I should do the assassination
but I did it anyway

I did it without you Nicholas
and I did it better than you
I did it a lot better

STAVROGIN.
I'm not the leader

PETER VERKHOVENSKY.
Yes Nicholas I understand that
but I need the money now
If I don't have the money
I won't be able to pay Kirilov
and Kirilov is the one who's going to take responsibility

STAVROGIN.
I'm not the

PETER VERKHOVENSKY.
Stop saying that
The Third Department might be here any minute

DASHA'S VOICE. *(On the other side of the door.)*
NICHOLAS ARE YOU ALL RIGHT

STAVROGIN.
Dasha

DASHA'S VOICE.
NICHOLAS

MRS. STAVROGIN'S VOICE.
DASHA
WHAT'S ALL THE YELLING ABOUT

(Dasha hurries off. Peter opens the door, looks out, then locks it again.)

PETER VERKHOVENSKY.
I think her devotion to you is very sweet
and possibly pathological

>   but look out
>   She's cut from the same cloth as her brother

(Outside the sound of a fire wagon passing, bells jangling, horns blaring.)

>   I never told you Shatov spat on me
>   yes he did He actually spat on me
>   He hates me that's why
>   He hates Russia
>   He hates everything Russia wants to become

>   In fact I've come to the realization
>   that in order for Russia to be born
>   I have to get rid
>   of filthy little reactionaries like Shatov

STAVROGIN.
>   Dasha

(Stavrogin is climbing out of bed, heading for the door.)

PETER VERKHOVENSKY.
>   Don't be scared
>   I'm the only man in this entire country
>   who is capable of taking action

STAVROGIN.
>   DASHA

PETER VERKHOVENSKY.
>   GIVE ME THE MONEY

STAVROGIN.
>   GET AWAY

(Stavrogin is trying to unlock the door. Peter pulls him away. Stavrogin fights him, seizing him by the hair and throwing him on the ground. He runs back to the door and is trying to unlock it again, when Peter crawls after him, and grabs him by the ankle.)

PETER VERKHOVENSKY.
>   What are you going to do
>   Tell the Third Department about me
>   What will you do after that
>   Live in some monastery
>   for child-molesters

(Stavrogin rushes back to Peter. Peter pulls out his revolver and stops him. Pause. Peter opens the door, and walks out.)

Scene 2

Dawn. Shigalyov's room. More firebells. More rain. Virginsky is pacing. Shigalyov is drinking from a flask. Liputin playing solitaire.

SHIGALYOV.
    So Liputin
    how many other groups does Peter have
    One
    More than one

LIPUTIN.
    He'll get here as soon as he can

VIRGINSKY.
    It's the other group who killed her
    We're going to be arrested for what they did

SHIGALYOV.
    Sit down Virginsky
(To Liputin:)
    Of course Peter has other groups
    You think he's depending completely on us
    He's smarter than that
    The Society's smarter than that

VIRGINSKY.
    That's why that guy is still watching us
    Why is he still watching us
    IT'S RAINING AND HE DOESN'T EVEN HAVE AN
        UMBRELLA
    I MEAN WHAT'S WRONG WITH THAT GUY

SHIGALYOV.
    Shut up Virginsky

LIPUTIN.
> He'll get here as soon as he can

SHIGALYOV.
> That's where Peter is right now isn't he
> He's meeting with the other group

VIRGINSKY.
> He's not going to get here
> as long as that guy is watching us

SHIGALYOV.
> Maybe he's not meeting with the other group
> Maybe he's halfway to Moscow
> while we sit here and wait for him to show up
> Peter's smart, we're stupid
> We're going to get arrested for a murder we didn't commit

LIPUTIN.
> What amazes me is that you don't trust Peter
> but you do trust Nicholas Stavrogin
> Nicholas Stavrogin who couldn't be bothered
> to answer our letters
> who still won't tell us why he quit the group
>
> Ask Nicholas Stavrogin why he quit the group
> But you won't do that, will you
> because you don't want to know the answer

VIRGINSKY.
> **WE'RE FUCKED**
> **WE'RE COMPLETELY AND IRRETRIEVABLY FUCKED**

SHIGALYOV.
> Have a drink Virginsky

(Shigalyov hands his flask to Virginsky, who takes a big drink. Liputin hits Shigalyov.)
> What did I do

LIPUTIN.
> When you get upset
> he gets upset

(Shigalyov takes a big drink.)

SHIGALYOV.
>   I'm not saying Peter's going to turn us in
>   to the Third Department
>   It would be stupid if he did
>   We could tell the Third Department all about him

VIRGINSKY. *(To Liputin.)*
>   We should turn you in to the Third Department
>   He tells you everything

SHIGALYOV.
>   And then Liputin will turn us in to the Third Department

LIPUTIN.
>   I wouldn't do that

SHIGALYOV.
>   Yes you would
>   You don't even like us

LIPUTIN.
>   Yes I do

SHIGALYOV.
>   Then maybe it's me you don't like

VIRGINSKY.
>   DESPOTS
>   THEY'RE ALL DESPOTS

(The sound of a distant explosion.)

SHIGALYOV.
>   That was the factory
>   Don't stand in the window Virginsky
>   Get out of the window

(Virginsky moves away from the window and starts kicking the wall.)

VIRGINSKY.
>   WE DIDN'T DO IT
>   WE DIDN'T DO IT
>   WE DIDN'T DO IT

SHIGALYOV.
>   Virginsky slow down

You're going to give yourself a heart attack
(But Virginsky's not listening, he's pacing faster and faster, bumping into walls, back and forth, back and forth.)

LIPUTIN.
>I read in the paper this morning
>There was an article in the paper
>about a private in the Moscow regiment
>and the private in the Moscow regiment
>was standing at attention
>as they were having inspection
>and the sergeant
>or whoever he was
>came up in front of the private
>and suddenly
>for no reason at all
>he bit him

SHIGALYOV.
>The private bit the sergeant

LIPUTIN.
>No the sergeant bit the private
>Right in the face
>Right in the cheek

VIRGINSKY.
>I THINK WHAT EVERYONE IN THIS COUNTRY NEEDS IS A GOOD LONG REST

(Pause.)

SHIGALYOV.
>I'll tell you what I think:
>before we were born they divided us into two groups:
>nine-tenths in this group
>and one-tenth in that group
>
>The nine-tenths group is us
>The herd
>the stinking animals of the world
>and we've always behaved with stinking obedience
>Generations of stinking obedience
>Oceans of vast boundless infinitely stinking obedience

The one-tenth group is the owners
Those people can have whatever they want
They can do whatever they want
They are the order-givers
We are the order-takers

Face it:
Nine-tenths of us are nothing but slaves
and will never be anything more than slaves
and must learn to be satisfied with slavery

Scene 3

Shatov's room. Marie is panting.

MARIE.
God in heaven

SHATOV.
Marie I think we should talk about this

MARIE.
I don't need a doctor

SHATOV.
But I don't think I can do this by myself

MARIE.
I'm the one who's doing it

(Stavrogin climbs the stairs to Shatov's apartment. Go To: Kirilov writing in his journal.)

KIRILOV'S VOICE.
There are two kinds of people who kill themselves. Those who don't think about it, and those who do. Those who don't think about it are the ones who kill themselves because they're sorry, or they're angry, or whatever. They do it suddenly, and they don't think about the pain.

But the ones who do think about it, they're doing it for a reason. They can't stop thinking about the reason, and

they can't stop thinking about the pain, either. That's the way it is. Most people are in the first group, and less people are in the second group. But if it weren't for prejudice on the part of society, there would be a lot more people in the second group.
(Stavrogin knocks at Shatov's door.)

SHATOV.
    Who is it

STAVROGIN.
    Nicholas Stavrogin
(Shatov opens the door a crack. Stavrogin enters. Marie pulls her blankets around herself.)

SHATOV.
    What do you want

STAVROGIN.
    Hello Marie
    I thought you were still in Geneva

MARIE.
    Well I'm not

STAVROGIN.
    Listen Shatov
    I'm not here to make peace with you
    I'm here to warn you that Peter might try to kill you

SHATOV.
    What do you mean

STAVROGIN.
    Exactly what I said
    You must have expected it

SHATOV.
    No

STAVROGIN.
    Well it's true

SHATOV.
    So what I'm not afraid of him
    You quit

So did I
I have the right to quit
Nobody on earth can take that away from me

You're doing this for Peter, aren't you
You're trying to scare me into giving back the press
You've probably got him out there on the stairs
     eavesdropping
Don't you
Don't you

STAVROGIN.
    Keep it down

SHATOV.
    Kirilov's been spying on me too
    He tried to kill me when we were in Chicago
    NEXT TIME I'LL BE THE ONE TO KILL HIM

STAVROGIN.
    Stop it Stop it
    I want to ask you something

SHATOV.
    Who are you to ask me anything
    You didn't answer my letters for two years

STAVROGIN.
    Peter says you're about to go to the Third Department
    and inform on him
    Is that true

SHATOV.
    No of course it's not true
    It's always a death sentence with him
    and it's all done on Society documents
    on papers sealed with Society seals
    So now he believes I'm dangerous
    Let him

STAVROGIN.
    You're not going to the Third Department

SHATOV.
>   You're in more trouble than I am

STAVROGIN.
>   Listen I'm trying to tell you

SHATOV.
>   Nicholas Stavrogin:
>   Do you believe in God
>
>   Nicholas Stavrogin I'm asking you:
>   Do you believe in God

STAVROGIN.
>   Do you?

SHATOV.
>   I asked you first

STAVROGIN.
>   Do you believe in God

SHATOV.
>   I believe in Russia
>   I believe in the Russian Orthodox Church
>   I believe in the Holy Spirit
>   I believe that the Second Coming will take place in Russia

STAVROGIN.
>   I'm going

SHATOV.
>   I WILL believe in God

(Stavrogin starts to go. Shatov grabs him by the sleeve.)
>   It doesn't matter whether I believe in God
>   It matters whether YOU believe in God
>   Whoever wants to save Russia must believe in God first

STAVROGIN.
>   Nobody can save Russia

(Shatov spits at him.)
>   For the last time
>   I'm telling you

>   They're going to try to kill you

SHATOV.
>   You ought to be begging me for forgiveness
>   You ought to be getting down on your knees
>   and begging me
>   kissing my feet for forgiveness

(Stavrogin heads down the stairs.)
>   You can't do this to me
>   You can't leave me like this
>   I've worshipped you
>   The whole time you were gone
>   I waited for you like a woman
>   like a woman I waited for you
>   but I wasn't ashamed
>   and I wasn't ashamed
>   because I was waiting for
>   THE GREAT AND TERRIBLE NICHOLAS STAVROGIN
>
>   I CAN'T TEAR YOU OUT OF MY HEART
>   NICHOLAS STAVROGIN

(Stavrogin runs away. From the shadows, someone is watching.)

Scene 4

>   *Mrs. Stavrogin's hall. Mrs. Stavrogin writes in her checkbook, as Stepan Verkhovensky watches. Dasha is in the background, folding laundry.*

MRS. STAVROGIN.
>   I'm giving you five thousand now
>   plus a check for two thousand which you can cash
>   next month
>
>   Thereafter you will receive a check from me
>   every other month in the amount of four thousand
>   It's not too little is it

(She tears off one check, then the second check, and hands them to him.)

STEPAN VERKHOVENSKY.
>   You expect this to replace
>   years of research
>   the most intimate look ever at the Golden Age
>   a major work which would have been a prized addition
>   to the collection of any bibliophile

MRS. STAVROGIN.
>   I don't care if it does or doesn't
>   I have given you two checks
>   I will also give you a statement in writing
>
>   plus the apartment in St. Petersburg
>   servants Take Dasha too if you like
>   You can convert it all to cash I don't care
>
>   I consider it my sacred duty
>   to continue your financial allowance
>   until your dying day
>
>   In special emergencies of course
>   I will let you have
>   more money

STEPAN VERKHOVENSKY.
>   I humbled myself before you
>   I carried your groceries
>   I took out your garbage
>   I sat in your salon
>   allowing you to introduce me as your tutor

MRS. STAVROGIN.
>   Don't tell me about tutors
>   Five years ago I asked you to marry me
>   I asked YOU
>   and you treated me
>   like I was your servant

STEPAN VERKHOVENSKY.
>   You never asked me to marry you

MRS. STAVROGIN.
>   I did

    I did
(She stops, and waits until Dasha is gone.)
    Believe me what you call
    romance
    is not exactly attractive

STEPAN VERKHOVENSKY.
    Ah *mon amour*

MRS. STAVROGIN.
    French is a reactionary language

STEPAN VERKHOVENSKY.
    French is the language of love

MRS. STAVROGIN.
    That was twenty years ago

STEPAN VERKHOVENSKY.
    You are the same woman I met twenty years ago

MRS. STAVROGIN.
    You are not the same man

STEPAN VERKHOVENSKY.
    You are the only person I have never betrayed
    Everyone else Yes
    at one point or another but not you

MRS. STAVROGIN.
    STOP IT STOP IT
    You betrayed me the night they arrested you
    You pointed your finger at me and said
    She made me do it
    She made me do it

STEPAN VERKHOVENSKY.
    I did not

MRS. STAVROGIN.
    DON'T LIE TO ME
    GOD DON'T LIE TO ME NOW
    That night
    we lost whatever connection we'd ever had

STEPAN VERKHOVENSKY.
    All right maybe I did
    but it was a moment of weakness
    I am only a human being

MRS. STAVROGIN.
    You're a coward
    You were a coward then
    and you're a coward now

STEPAN VERKHOVENSKY.
    So this is it
    This is the end
    after twenty years

MRS. STAVROGIN.
    Twenty years of
    your pompous CONCEIT
    You're a stylist
    not a lover
    Your love poems are nothing more than
    a glorified expression of slops

STEPAN VERKHOVENSKY.
    Slops
    oh that's erudite

MRS. STAVROGIN.
    They took your books and papers by MISTAKE
    can't you see that?
    You're not worth arresting You're NOTHING

    They wanted to arrest your SON
    He's the one who's got a future
    He's the one who's got something to live for

    You have nothing
    Nobody cares what you say or think
    Tales from Spanish History

    Who cares about history
    when the world is falling down around our ears
    A jug is useful because you can pour water into it

> An apple is beautiful because you can eat it
> A real woman's face is more beautiful
> than any Mona Lisa you can name

STEPAN VERKHOVENSKY.
> And so are you
> You're beautiful

MRS. STAVROGIN.
> TOO LATE TOO LATE
> You only care about yourself and your headaches
> and your bowels
> Your disgusting bowels

STEPAN VERKHOVENSKY.
> So you're saying you despise me

MRS. STAVROGIN.
> Yes

STEPAN VERKHOVENSKY.
> And at this moment you feel nothing but disgust
>   for me

MRS. STAVROGIN.
> YESSSS

STEPAN VERKHOVENSKY.
> Well if that's the way you want it
>
> But I shall be a true knight
> I shall remain faithful at least
> to the concept of love
>
> Yes I have sponged off you
> Yes I am weak
> but I was never a criminal
>
> and I always loved you
> From now on
> I shall accept nothing from you
>
> Take your checks back

(He drops the checks on the floor.)

MRS. STAVROGIN.
    Good

STEPAN VERKHOVENSKY.
    Au revoir my dreams
    Good-bye twenty years of happiness
    Alea Jacta Est

MRS. STAVROGIN.
    I HATE LATIN

STEPAN VERKHOVENSKY.
    Alea Jacta Est

MRS. STAVROGIN.
    You'll always be a beggar
    a BUM
    THE TOWN BUM

STEPAN VERKHOVENSKY.
    Alea Jacta Est
(He leaves. She runs to her room, sobbing. Pause. Peter emerges from the closet. He picks up the checks, and leaves.)

Scene 5

Dawn. Lembke's salon. Lembke sits, hugging his wife's dress.

BLUM.
    You've only got ten firemen in this entire town
    You've lost most of your docks
    and half your warehouses are on fire
    I say let your docks go
    and concentrate on your warehouses
    If you can't control your warehouses
    all your shacks are going to be next

LEMBKE.
    What about the rain

BLUM.
>The rain's not going to put this fire out
>and you can't use the police either
>You need the police for crowd-control

LEMBKE.
>Maybe the Third Department

BLUM.
>The Third Department's not going to fight a fire for you
>Listen
>I'm not responsible
>I refuse to be responsible
>If this town burns down it will be your own fault

LEMBKE.
>But you don't understand Mister Blum
>The fire out there
>That's not the real fire
>The real fire is in here

(Tapping his forehead with his finger.)
>The fire's in here

Scene 6

Stepan Verkhovensky stumbles out of the house to discover Dasha, huddled on the ground. It is raining.

STEPAN VERKHOVENSKY.
>Who's that

DASHA.
>DON'T COME NEAR ME
>I WON'T GO WITH YOU
>I WON'T GO WITH YOU

STEPAN VERKHOVENSKY.
>Mademoiselle I would never in my wildest dreams

DASHA.
>DON'T MAKE ME GO
>I'LL KILL MYSELF IF YOU MAKE ME GO

STEPAN VERKHOVENSKY.
Mademoiselle nobody's making you go anywhere

DASHA.
I'LL NEVER FORGIVE HER
NEVER

STEPAN VERKHOVENSKY.
Get off your knees
It doesn't matter if you can forgive her or not
Miss Dasha for your information
You are now officially
on your own

DASHA.
No

STEPAN VERKHOVENSKY.
Yes you are
We are each going into the world this morning
and you must fare for yourself

DASHA.
Stop Stop
Before you go just tell me one thing:
Is it true

STEPAN VERKHOVENSKY.
Yes
After twenty years it's over
but I'll be all right I'm a lot stronger than I look

DASHA.
No the Governor's wife
Is it true about the Governor's wife

STEPAN VERKHOVENSKY.
Mrs. Lembke

DASHA.
He poisoned her didn't he
He told his friends to poison her

STEPAN VERKHOVENSKY.
> Say why don't we run away together
> I'm running away to find the real Russia
> Of course it's a question as to whether Russia exists
> but never mind
> I always knew I'd come across a beautiful woman like you
> and together we'd go off on a wild adventure

DASHA.
> I don't want to go away

STEPAN VERKHOVENSKY.
> All right then Don't
> Go back to Nicholas if that's what you want
> I'll go by myself
> I'm going to find the real Russia
> the one with the serfs
> and good and kindly people who adopt orphan babies
> and innocent girls who give up too much for love

DASHA.
> No Wait Mister Verkhovensky Please

STEPAN VERKHOVENSKY.
> Ah there's nothing like the sound of a woman saying Please

(She makes the sign of the cross over him.)

DASHA.
> The Lord bless you and keep you

STEPAN VERKHOVENSKY.
> Don't cling to me
> This is nothing more than emotional slops

(He pushes her away.)

> "Love is the crown of human existence."
> Who said THAT?

(He staggers into the rain. She watches him go.)

Scene 7

Shigalyov's room. Shigalyov, Virginsky, and Liputin stand as Peter Verkhovensky enters with his briefcase.

PETER VERKHOVENSKY.
> Sit down

SHIGALYOV.
> Where have you been
> We've been sitting here since last night
> with our thumbs up our asses

PETER VERKHOVENSKY.
> I've been busy

SHIGALYOV.
> Busy shit
> Virginsky's quitting
> and so am I

LIPUTIN.
> You can't quit unless we give you permission

VIRGINSKY.
> Shatov quit

SHIGALYOV.
> Granny has quit too hasn't he

LIPUTIN.
> If anyone else quits we'll all have to quit

PETER VERKHOVENSKY.
> Before you all quit
> you might want to know something:
> A friend of mine who works at the Third Department
> intercepted this
>
> It's from Shatov
> Evidently he thinks you're the ones
> who killed the Governor's wife
> I'm afraid Shatov has gone completely over the edge

(Peter Verkhovensky pulls a letter from his briefcase, and gives it to Liputin.)

LIPUTIN. *(Reading aloud.)*
   To Whom It May Concern There is a grop

PETER VERKHOVENSKY.
   Group

LIPUTIN. *(Reading aloud.)*
   of terrorists in our town bent of wrecking havoc and burning down the system stupid but worse total nihilists running with their eyes bugging out THEY ARE THE ONES KILLED THE GOVERNOR'S WIFE If you want more information put a light on your first floor window tomorrow night I will come to you but on condition I get a pardon from the Governor and I get a pension too Signed, A Repentant Freethinker Anonymous

VIRGINSKY.
   WE DIDN'T KILL HER

SHIGALYOV.
   What the hell is this

LIPUTIN. *(Reading aloud.)*
   P.S. Nicholas Stavrogin is a nymphomaniac

PETER VERKHOVENSKY.
   I suspected this might happen
   so I've been having him watched

VIRGINSKY.
   BUT WE DIDN'T KILL HER

LIPUTIN.
   Shut up Virginsky

PETER VERKHOVENSKY.
   I know Virginsky
   but Shatov doesn't care about the truth
   I wouldn't be surprised if he also tells them
   you're the ones who set the fire

VIRGINSKY.
   WHY IS HE DOING THIS

SHIGALYOV.
> So Shatov is going to the Third Department
> That little shit

LIPUTIN.
> Suddenly I'm not surprised

SHIGALYOV.
> Neither am I

LIPUTIN.
> He wants to pin it all on us

PETER VERKHOVENSKY.
> If I were you, I'd think about leaving town
> I'd go to St. Petersburg or better yet Moscow
> Though I don't know how you'll get there
> until the strike is over

LIPUTIN.
> Shit Shit Shit

SHIGALYOV.
> So he's going to get off scot-free
> while we have to run away and hide

VIRGINSKY.
> But it's not fair

PETER VERKHOVENSKY.
> That's what I like about you Virginsky
> You're always concerned with what's fair

VIRGINSKY.
> I don't like it when people turn on their friends

LIPUTIN.
> If he were our friend
> he wouldn't do this to us

SHIGALYOV.
> I say Fuck him
> He started it
> Let's give him what he deserves

VIRGINSKY.
> What do you mean

SHIGALYOV.
>   We should have done it a long time ago

PETER VERKHOVENSKY.
>   Are you saying what I think you're saying

SHIGALYOV.
>   I'm saying let's send him to hell

LIPUTIN.
>   We're only protecting ourselves

PETER VERKHOVENSKY.
>   But he's a member of your own group

LIPUTIN.
>   He's going to the Third Department tomorrow night

PETER VERKHOVENSKY.
>   Are you thinking about doing it tonight

VIRGINSKY.
>   Tonight?

SHIGALYOV.
>   I think he's right
>   If we're going to do something
>   we'd better do it fast

LIPUTIN.
>   I guess we could do it tonight

PETER VERKHOVENSKY.
>   If you did it late
>   say around three o'clock

SHIGALYOV.
>   Tonight is too late

PETER VERKHOVENSKY.
>   You can't do it in broad daylight

LIPUTIN.
>   No we can't do it in broad daylight

PETER VERKHOVENSKY.
>   One of you will have to go to his room

SHIGALYOV.
　　Virginsky

VIRGINSKY.
　　Me

LIPUTIN.
　　He likes you

SHIGALYOV.
　　Tell him we want him to give back the press

VIRGINSKY.
　　It's a shitty press

PETER VERKHOVENSKY.
　　You don't care about the press

SHIGALYOV.
　　Make him take you to where he buried it

LIPUTIN.
　　We'll meet you there
　　When you get there
　　whistle
　　so we'll know it's you

VIRGINSKY.
　　Wait
　　Wait
　　I don't know if I
　　I don't think I can do this

(Pause.)

LIPUTIN.
　　What do you mean

VIRGINSKY.
　　I don't know
　　I just
　　I don't think I can do this

LIPUTIN.
　　Shatov is accusing you of murder

SHIGALYOV.
　　Tomorrow night it will be too late

VIRGINSKY.
> I know but

LIPUTIN.
> Virginsky a minute ago you were all for it
> Are you changing your mind

VIRGINSKY.
> No I
> No but

(Pause. He looks to Shigalyov.)

SHIGALYOV.
> All right then

LIPUTIN.
> Let's do it

Scene 8

> *Shatov's room. Shatov tries to feed a piece of bread to Marie, who is lying in bed, groaning.*

MARIE.
> Ivan Ivan

SHATOV.
> I'm here my darling what can I do

MARIE.
> Get that bread out of my face
> You're making me sick

SHATOV.
> Maybe I should get a doctor

MARIE.
> Ivan

SHATOV.
> What

MARIE.
> I've been thinking about
> starting a publishing business
> Ivan since you live here

what's your opinion:
Do you think it would have a chance OH GOD

SHATOV.
I don't know, Marie
Are you talking about books or a newspaper
(She grits her teeth and goes through another wave of pain.)

MARIE.
Talk to me Talk to me TALK TO ME

SHATOV.
Marie Marie if I could only tell you how glad I am to see you
This place
these people
I'm surrounded by old-fashioned liberals
who are afraid of their own independence
FLUNKEYS Marie flunkeys to the old ideas
(She groans.)
What they need is a God a real God
not anybody else's God but their own God
but all they think about is politics and more politics
POLITICS HAS NOTHING TO DO WITH REASON
GOD IS REASON
GOD IS FREEDOM
IF I DIDN'T BELIEVE IN GOD I'D GO CRAZY

MARIE.
Help me

SHATOV.
Oh God Marie
Let me get a doctor PLEASE

MARIE.
NO I DON'T WANT TO BE ALONE
DON'T LEAVE ME ALONE

SHATOV.
I won't I won't
I'll just be gone a few
but I've got to talk to somebody

I'll be right back Marie
I'll be right back I promise
(He grabs his coat.)

MARIE.
DON'T LEAVE ME
SHATOV
SHATOV

(He throws himself out the door. A figure is coming up the stairs.)

VIRGINSKY.
Shatov

SHATOV.
I can't talk to you right now
My wife is having a baby

VIRGINSKY.
Shatov they've agreed to let you go
but you have to hand over the printing press first

SHATOV.
I can't talk about this now

VIRGINSKY.
You have to

SHATOV.
I'll talk about it tomorrow

VIRGINSKY.
Not tomorrow
We have to talk about it now

SHATOV.
Why now

VIRGINSKY.
Because
they want you to hand it over tonight
at three o'clock

SHATOV.
Three o'clock in the morning

VIRGINSKY.
    Yes

SHATOV.
    Why do we have to do it
    at three o'clock in the morning

VIRGINSKY.
    Because
    Because that's the only time they can do it

SHATOV.
    I'll do it tomorrow in the afternoon

VIRGINSKY.
    They can't do it in the afternoon
    It has to be dark
    so nobody can see us

(Pause.)

SHATOV.
    Okay
    but I'll only do it with you
    Not them, you hear me
    Only you

VIRGINSKY.
    Fine

(Marie cries out.)

SHATOV.
    I'VE GOT TO GO

VIRGINSKY.
    Wait I forgot to ask

SHATOV.
    What

VIRGINSKY.
    Where did you bury it

SHATOV.
    In the park

VIRGINSKY.
    Where in the park

SHATOV.
>By the pond

VIRGINSKY.
>Fine
>I'll come back for you at two-thirty

SHATOV.
>Will Peter be there

VIRGINSKY.
>Peter has left town

SHATOV.
>You mean he's run away
>Well that's a kick in the head for you

VIRGINSKY.
>I'll be here at two-thirty

SHATOV.
>YOU'RE A LITTLE FOOL VIRGINSKY

(Shatov runs away. Virginsky runs away. Far above, Marie cries out. Kirilov sticks his head out of his room, and listens.)

MARIE.
>SOMEBODY HELP ME

(Slowly, Kirilov starts to climb the stairs.)

Scene 9

Mrs. Stavrogin's house. Shatov arrives, throwing himself against the door, and kicking it.

SHATOV.
>DASHA DASHA OPEN THE DOOR
>OPEN THE DOOR
>OPEN THE DOOR

(Dasha comes to the other side of the door. She doesn't open it.)

DASHA.
>I don't have any money Ivan

SHATOV.
> I NEED YOU RIGHT NOW
> RIGHT NOW MY WIFE IS HAVING A BABY

DASHA.
> Your wife

SHATOV.
> YES RIGHT NOW
> YOU'VE GOT TO COME

DASHA.
> You mean Marie

SHATOV.
> YES RIGHT NOW
> COME WITH ME
> OR I'LL SCREAM EVEN LOUDER

DASHA.
> Marie has come back to you?

SHATOV.
> YES
> WILL YOU COME
> YOU'VE GOT TO COME NOW
> INSTANTLY

(Mrs. Stavrogin appears in the shadows.)

MRS. STAVROGIN.
> What's going on

DASHA.
> How long ago did she come back

SHATOV.
> YESTERDAY
> NO THE DAY BEFORE
> PLEASE
> HURRY

MRS. STAVROGIN.
> I thought she was in Switzerland

DASHA.
> Why does she want me

MRS. STAVROGIN.
> Don't do it

SHATOV.
> DASHAAAA

DASHA.
> All right Ivan
> I'll be right out

SHATOV.
> I'LL MEET YOU DOWN THERE
> I'VE GOT TO BUY SOME THINGS
> GO THERE GO RIGHT AWAY
> GO RIGHT NOW

(Shatov runs away.)

Scene 10

> *Night. Shatov runs down one set of stairs and up another, arriving at Liputin's door. He bangs on it.*

SHATOV.
> LIPUTIN OPEN THE DOOR
> IT'S ME
> LIPUTIN OPEN THE DOOR

LIPUTIN'S VOICE. *(In a whisper.)*
> What are you doing here

SHATOV.
> Come to the window
> I want to borrow some money
> I'll pay you back

LIPUTIN'S VOICE.
> I'll scream
> And the police will come and they'll arrest you

SHATOV.
> Well then I'll scream too
> You're more scared of the police than I am

(Liputin opens the shutter.)

LIPUTIN.
>All right keep your voice down
>Jesus Christ Almighty
>What do you want money for

SHATOV.
>My wife has come back
>and she's having a baby
>I've got to buy some supplies

LIPUTIN.
>Your wife

SHATOV.
>Yes isn't it wonderful

LIPUTIN.
>I thought she was in Geneva

SHATOV.
>I need to borrow some money

LIPUTIN.
>Okay fine
>but I don't think I have any money
>Let me think

SHATOV.
>You damned miser
>If you don't give me some money
>I'll start screaming and the police will come

LIPUTIN.
>All right here's five
>Scream all you like
>Scream the house down
>You won't get any more than that from me

SHATOV.
>To hell with you
>I ought to break every bone in your body

LIPUTIN.
>That's it Shatov

    Resort to violence
    That will get you what you want
SHATOV.
    Asshole
(Shatov runs off.)
LIPUTIN.
    THAT'S EXACTLY WHY YOU'RE IN THE TROUBLE YOU'RE IN

Scene 11

Kirilov stands on the dark landing, listening to Marie in terror, as she screams again and again. Dasha climbs slowly up the stairs.

DASHA.
    Sure is dark up here
KIRILOV.
    She keeps screaming
DASHA.
    Have you ever done this before
KIRILOV.
    Not me
    Haven't you
DASHA.
    No of course not
    Don't go
KIRILOV.
    I wouldn't be any help to you
(Kirilov hurries down the stairs. Dasha goes to the door of Shatov's room.)
MARIE.
    Who's there
DASHA.
    It's Dasha

MARIE.
>Go away

DASHA.
>I've come to help you

MARIE.
>Go away
>Leave me alone

DASHA.
>He told me to come
>but if you don't want me
>all right

MARIE.
>No
>Don't go
>Don't go
>Please
>Just don't let me die
>I don't want to die

(Shatov enters with supplies, out of breath.)

SHATOV.
>I'm back my darling

MARIE.
>>DON'T COME IN HERE
>>STAND IN THE CORNER
>>WITH YOUR FACE TO THE WALL

(Shatov puts the bag down. He goes to the corner and stands with his face to the wall.)

DASHA.
>Now let's see what we've got here

MARIE.
>I want to comb my hair

DASHA.
>Right now

MARIE.
>>I WANT TO COMB MY HAIR

>   GIVE ME MY COMB
>   I WANT IT

DASHA.
>   Don't you think you should

MARIE.
>   GET ME MY COMB

DASHA.
>   All right all right
>   Is it in here
> *(She picks up Marie's purse.)*

MARIE.
>   NOT YOU
>   HIM
>   DON'T OPEN MY BAG
>   ONLY HIM
>   I WANT HIM TO DO IT

DASHA.
>   Don't cry
>   Don't cry
>   Everything's going to be fine
>   You're going to be just fine
> *(Dasha hands the bag to Shatov. He finds a comb, and hands it to Dasha, who starts combing Marie's hair.)*

SHATOV.
>   I'll be downstairs

DASHA.
>   Where are you going

SHATOV.
>   I'll be in Kirilov's room
>   If you need me just yell

DASHA.
>   Ivan
> *(Shatov goes out, and slowly climbs down the stairs into Kirilov's room. Kirilov is cutting into a loaf of bread. He looks up.)*

SHATOV.
>   Kirilov my wife is having a baby
>   She's giving birth to a baby

KIRILOV.
>   I wish I could give birth
>   It must be wonderful
>   Life

SHATOV.
>   You know Kirilov
>   if you could learn to believe in God
>   you'd be a lot happier

KIRILOV.
>   Listen
>   I'll let you have some of this bread
>   but you have to promise not to talk okay
>   No Talking

Scene 12

Kirilov's room. Shatov sits at the table, as Kirilov lights a lantern.

MARIE'S VOICE.
>   HELP ME
>   HELP ME SOMEBODY
>   SOMEBODY HELP ME

(Shatov bolts out of the room, and runs up the stairs. Kirilov follows him as far as the door, when Liputin jumps out of the shadows.)

LIPUTIN.
>   What's Shatov doing in your room

KIRILOV.
>   What do you want

LIPUTIN.
>   I've been trying to deliver a message
>   but you kept going upstairs
>   and coming downstairs
>   and now you've been talking to HIM

MARIE'S VOICE.
    GET AWAY FROM ME
SHATOV'S VOICE.
    MARIE
DASHA'S VOICE.
    DON'T TOUCH HER
SHATOV'S VOICE.
    BUT MARIE
MARIE'S VOICE.
    NOOOOOO
DASHA'S VOICE.
    OH GOD HERE IT COMES
(Suddenly, silence.)
LIPUTIN.
    He's trying to turn us in to the Third Department you
        know
KIRILOV.
    Shatov
LIPUTIN.
    But we're not going to let him
    We're not afraid anymore
    not of him Not of anyone
KIRILOV.
    Oh really
LIPUTIN.
    Yes really
    Can you be ready tonight
KIRILOV.
    Why
LIPUTIN.
    Tonight
    3 o'clock
    You're going to do it tonight

KIRILOV.
> I guess

LIPUTIN.
> You're not going to chicken out are you

KIRILOV.
> No

LIPUTIN.
> Good
> Here's your stinking five hundred

(Liputin hands him an envelope, and runs away. In the distance, the sound of an explosion. Bells of a fire engine. Flames, crackling.)

Scene 13

Above, Shatov's landing is full of moonlight. Shatov is inside, watching Dasha wrap a baby in rags. She gives the baby to Marie, and covers them both with the blanket.

DASHA.
> See
> It's a boy
> You can tell by the silly expression on its face

SHATOV.
> This is a great
> This is a great joy to me
> The mystery of a new human being
> is such a complete and utter mystery

DASHA.
> Thanks
> Are you going to keep him

SHATOV.
> Of course I'm going to keep him
> Why wouldn't I

(Dasha gives him a kiss, and leaves. Shatov goes over to Marie, and leans over, looking at her. She looks dead. He looks closer. She opens her eyes.)

MARIE.
> Ivan

SHATOV.
>Don't hit me

MARIE.
>Bend over
>More
>A little more
>A little more

(She puts her arm around his neck, brings his forehead down to her lips, and kisses it.)

SHATOV.
>Marie

(He sinks onto the bed beside her, and they embrace. Downstairs: Kirilov sits bolt upright. He goes to the door, and opens it a crack. Outside, he sees a figure creeping quietly up the stairs. The figure arrives at Shatov's door, and looks in. Elsewhere, Dasha turns with a scream.)

DASHA.
>IVANNNNNNN

(Shatov opens his eyes. Virginsky is standing in the door, carrying a lantern and a shovel.)

SHATOV. *(In a whisper:)*
>What do you want

VIRGINSKY.
>Are you ready

SHATOV.
>Don't come in
>Wait for me downstairs

(Virginsky goes. Shatov grabs his coat and cap, and follows him.)
>I'd forgotten all about you

VIRGINSKY.
>Hurry up

SHATOV.
>Virginsky wait
>Virginsky wait
>It's a boy

Scene 14

The park at night. Shigalyov and Liputin stand with lanterns. A third lantern approaches. It's Peter.

PETER VERKHOVENSKY.
    Is that you Liputin
    What's the matter, are you sick

LIPUTIN.
    I'm not sick

PETER VERKHOVENSKY.
    So is Virginsky the only one not here

LIPUTIN.
    Shatov's wife has come back to him
    and she's in labour

PETER VERKHOVENSKY.
    So

LIPUTIN.
    So
    I think it's safe to say
    Shatov is happy
    happier
    and if he's happier
    maybe he won't go to the Third Department

PETER VERKHOVENSKY.
    That doesn't make sense
    Just because a person is happy
    doesn't mean he'll hold back
    from doing something he thinks is right

LIPUTIN.
    That's not what I mean

PETER VERKHOVENSKY.
    I know she's back So what
    I don't know why Shatov should be so happy

>   to see his wife come back
>   giving birth to another man's child

SHIGALYOV.
>   I'd like to say something too

PETER VERKHOVENSKY.
>   So say it

SHIGALYOV.
>   I think
>   when he gets here
>   we ought to be honest and ask him straight out
>   just ask him
>   if he's going to the Third Department
>   and if he is
>   we ought to make him apologize
>   and give his word of honor
>   that he won't
>   and then we ought to let him go

LIPUTIN.
>   Right That's what I say

PETER VERKHOVENSKY.
>   Let's lower our voices shall we
>   or we'll miss the signal
>   Shatov
>   gentlemen
>
>   thinks you poisoned the Governor's wife
>   None of you has the right
>   to stake the life of the Society
>   much less the lives of your fellow-members
>
>   on the ravings
>   of a maniac
>   in addition to which
>   the Third Department isn't going to drop the charges
>
>   no matter what you tell them
>   Even if you're acquitted of the murder

they'll still get you for conspiracy to overthrow the
    Government

SHIGALYOV.
   I'm not going to do this
   I refuse to take part in this whole thing
   I'm going home

PETER VERKHOVENSKY.
   Are you going to the Third Department

SHIGALYOV.
   No
(Suddenly, a whistle from the dark. Everybody freezes. Peter whistles back.)

PETER VERKHOVENSKY.
   Here he comes
(Peter, Shigalyov, and Liputin step back into darkness, as Virginsky appears with Shatov.)

SHATOV.
   Don't worry
   No one can hear us all the way out here
   We'd have to fire a cannon for them to hear us

   This is the place
   right here
   about two feet down
(Shatov stamps on the ground with his foot.)

PETER VERKHOVENSKY.
   NOW
(Peter rushes out of the dark, and shoves his revolver up against Shatov's head. Shatov turns and looks at him, then at Liputin and Shigalyov as they come out of the dark.)
   Hit him

SHATOV.
   What the

PETER VERKHOVENSKY.
   Hit him

(Shigalyov slugs Shatov in the face.)
>HARDER

VIRGINSKY.
>NOOO

(Peter fires.)

SHIGALYOV.
>Oh God we've done it now

(Liputin lets the body slump to the ground.)

LIPUTIN.
>This is all wrong
>This is all wrong

(Peter is stooping over the body, going through its pockets. He finds nothing, and straightens.)

PETER VERKHOVENSKY.
>Hurry up

(Liputin and Shigalyov run off into the darkness, and return, carrying two enormous stones. Virginsky and Peter tie ropes around the body's neck and feet, and then tie the ropes to the stones. Shigalyov stands there, hunched over, still holding his stone.)

VIRGINSKY.
>You can put it down now Shigalyov

SHIGALYOV.
>Put it down

(Shigalyov puts the stone down. They finish tying the ropes. Suddenly Liputin explodes:)

LIPUTIN.
>BUT IT'S ALL WRONG
>IT'S ALL WRONG
>IT'S ALL WRONG

(Shigalyov grabs Liputin from behind, squeezing him with all his strength.)

SHIGALYOV.
>SHUT UP

PETER VERKHOVENSKY.
>SHUT UP

LIPUTIN.
>IT'S ALL WRONG
>IT'S ALL WRONG

SHIGALYOV.
>STOP IT
>STOP IT
>STOP IT

PETER VERKHOVENSKY.
>SHUT UP

LIPUTIN.
>IT'S ALL WRONG

(Liputin turns on Peter and hits him in the face. Peter puts his revolver straight into Liputin's mouth.)

SHIGALYOV.
>Don't do it

(Peter takes the revolver out.)

VIRGINSKY.
>You didn't have to do that

PETER VERKHOVENSKY.
>Come on let's go

(They stoop and put the stones on the body's chest and legs. Picking up the body, they lug it into the darkness.)

>One
>Two
>Three

(A splash is heard, as the body is thrown into the pond. They return.)

>Gentlemen
>
>I'd like to say however
>here and now
>if you feel upset
>it's only natural
>and if you don't feel upset
>
>I'm sure you will in the next day or two.
>Remember
>the reason you joined this group

in the first place
was to act upon your beliefs.

You are men of principle.
Now then
I want everybody to leave separately
no groups please
Tomorrow I want you all to spend the day at home

LIPUTIN.
   I'm sorry

PETER VERKHOVENSKY.
   It's all right

LIPUTIN.
   I lost my head

PETER VERKHOVENSKY.
   I know
   Go on

LIPUTIN.
   I'm sorry

(Liputin hurries away. Virginsky hurries away.)

SHIGALYOV.
   Peter wait
   I want to know something
   Are we the only group you work with

PETER VERKHOVENSKY.
   I already told you

SHIGALYOV.
   I want to know

PETER VERKHOVENSKY.
   What possible difference could it make
   whether there are five of you
   or five thousand

SHIGALYOV.
   So you're telling me
   we're not the only ones

PETER VERKHOVENSKY.
> I'm not telling you anything

SHIGALYOV.
> I knew it
> I knew it all the time
> Thanks
> Thank you

(Shigalyov hurries away.)

Scene 15

Dasha standing at Mrs. Stavrogin's window, in the dark. A candle hurries in.

MRS. STAVROGIN.
> Did you hear that

DASHA.
> Down by the pond
> They were yelling something just a minute ago

MRS. STAVROGIN.
> Who is it

DASHA.
> I don't know
> I saw a light
> Now it's gone

MRS. STAVROGIN.
> Do you think we should send for the police

DASHA.
> I don't know
> Yes

MRS. STAVROGIN.
> But maybe we shouldn't
> If they find out
>   whoever they are

DASHA.
> Get the police

MRS. STAVROGIN.
>But if they find out that we sent for the police
>they might come after us
>whoever they are

(Dasha crosses to the door as:)
>We're alone now
>Anything could happen to us
>We've got nobody to take care of us
>nobody at all

DASHA.
>I'm going to get the police

MRS. STAVROGIN.
>A woman can't let them know she's alone in the world
>If they find out
>they go after her
>like a pack of wolves

(Dasha hurries out.)

Scene 16

Night. Kirilov is sitting at the table, staring at his revolver.

The door opens, and Peter enters.

KIRILOV.
>I was beginning to think you weren't coming

PETER VERKHOVENSKY.
>I know I'm late
>but on the other hand
>I've given you a present of two hours

KIRILOV.
>Stupid

(Pause.)

PETER VERKHOVENSKY.
>So what's going on
>Are we going to keep our promise

KIRILOV.
> I'm keeping it
> It's all the same to me

PETER VERKHOVENSKY.
> Good
> I'll dictate the letter to you
> and by the way
> I want to put in a part about Shatov

KIRILOV.
> Why Shatov

PETER VERKHOVENSKY.
> Why not

KIRILOV.
> His wife came back to him today
> In fact she had a baby

PETER VERKHOVENSKY.
> She can't hear us can she

KIRILOV.
> She can't hear anything
> and if Shatov comes
> you can hide in the other room

PETER VERKHOVENSKY.
> Shatov's not coming
> I want you to write that you had an argument with him tonight
> about him being a traitor and an informer
> and so you shot him

KIRILOV.
> I shot him

PETER VERKHOVENSKY.
> Yes

KIRILOV.
> Is he dead

PETER VERKHOVENSKY.
> Yes

KIRILOV.
> You killed him

PETER VERKHOVENSKY.
> His friends did

KIRILOV.
> I knew it
> I knew this was going to happen
> I knew it
> *(Peter has taken a revolver out of his pocket, and is keeping it low, on his lap.)*
> All this because he wanted to quit your little group

PETER VERKHOVENSKY.
> That's not true
> Shatov was out of control
> He's been out of control for some time
> but I don't have any hard feelings about him
> *(Peter stops, as Kirilov picks up his own gun from the chair, and aims it at Peter. Peter lifts his revolver and aims back.)*
> Oooooh
> Think how awful it would be
> if I pulled the trigger right now

KIRILOV.
> Fuck it
> I'm not going to write anything
> There's not going to be any letter
> You can all go fuck yourselves

PETER VERKHOVENSKY.
> I thought this would happen
> I had a feeling you wouldn't do it
> even though you promised
> even though you took money from us, and everything
>
> You're an ass Kirilov
> and if you're not going to blow your brains out
> I'll do it for you
> just like I did for Shatov
> *(Pause. Kirilov lowers his gun.)*

KIRILOV.
>	Tell me what to write
>	I'll write anything
>	I'll write that I killed Shatov
>	Hurry up
>
>	I'm not afraid of what you think
>	You're just a slave to your rebellion
>	You're going to be crushed before it's over
>	*(Kirilov seizes paper and pen, and starts to write.)*
>	I Alexei Kirilov declare

PETER VERKHOVENSKY.
>	Today
>	the 18th of November

KIRILOV.
>	Wait No
>	Who am I declaring to

PETER VERKHOVENSKY.
>	What do you mean

KIRILOV.
>	I want to know
>	Who am I declaring to

PETER VERKHOVENSKY.
>	To nobody
>	To the first person who reads it
>	To the whole world

KIRILOV.
>	I don't want any repentance
>	and I'm not doing this for the authorities

PETER VERKHOVENSKY.
>	To hell with the authorities
>	Go on
>	Do it

KIRILOV.
>	Go on
>	do it

I Alexei Kirilov declare today
the 18th of November

PETER VERKHOVENSKY.
Last night at ten o'clock
(As Kirilov writes, his voice goes on without him.)

KIRILOV'S VOICE.
Last night at ten o'clock I killed First Lady Mrs. Lembke at her house for committing treason against the great and glorious people.

PETER VERKHOVENSKY.
Our

KIRILOV.
Our great and glorious people.

KIRILOV'S VOICE.
Also in the park you will find the body of a man named Ivan Shatov. He was a traitor, too. I am shooting myself today with my own revolver not because I'm sorry for anything I've done, but because I made up my mind long ago to kill myself.

(Kirilov turns to Peter.)

KIRILOV.
Is that all

PETER VERKHOVENSKY.
That's all

KIRILOV.
Wait

PETER VERKHOVENSKY.
GIVE IT TO ME

KIRILOV.
I haven't signed it

PETER VERKHOVENSKY.
Sign it then

KIRILOV.
I want to tell them off but good

PETER VERKHOVENSKY.
 Vive la republique
KIRILOV.
 No that's wrong
 Give me liberty or give me death
PETER VERKHOVENSKY.
 That's great
 That's great
KIRILOV. *(Still signing.)*
 Alexei de Kiriloff
 gentleman
 citizen of the world
 and of the universe
PETER VERKHOVENSKY.
 All right
 Enough
 Stop
(Peter grabs the letter. Kirilov takes his revolver and runs out of the room. Silence. Candle in one hand, revolver in the other, Peter follows Kirilov, and finds him behind the door, rigid, his face pressed hard to the wall. He seems to be hiding.)
 Kirilov
 Kirilov
(Peter pushes his candle into Kirilov's face. Kirilov's eyes slide sideways, watching him.)
 What are you doing
(Kirilov knocks the candle out of Peter's hands. Peter goes down, striking back with his revolver.)
 DON'T
(Kirilov seizes Peter's hand and bites it, hard. Peter screams. Kirilov rushes back into his apartment and slams the door. Peter stays down, sucking on his hand. Suddenly, a gunshot. Peter walks back into the apartment. He relights the candle and holds it up, looking everywhere. Then he sees it — Kirilov's body in the corner, bleeding from the right temple, the gun still in its hand. He stares at the body a moment. He drops the letter on the floor nearby. He puts the candle on the table. <u>Upstairs</u>: Marie in Shatov's bed. She opens her eyes.)

MARIE.
>	Ivan

(She gets up, lays her coat over the baby, then creeps to the landing, and looks down the stairs into the dark.)
>	Ivan

(The sound of Peter running into the dark. His shadow flares against the wall.)
>	Ivan

(Marie slowly climbs down the stairs, holding onto the banister. Marie arrives at the bottom of the stairs. She crosses to Kirilov's door. It is open. She enters, and stands a moment in the near-dark, before she sees the body on the floor. She takes several steps towards it, and then realizes it's Kirilov.)
>	Kirilov

(She backs away from it, and hurries out of the room, pulling herself up the stairs as fast as she can.)
>	SOMEBODY
>	SOMEBODY HELP ME
>	HELP ME SOMEBODY
>	HELP ME
>	THEY'VE KILLED HIM
>	THEY'VE KILLED IVAN
>	THEY'VE KILLED IVAN

(At the same time: Shigalyov's room. Virginsky hides in one corner. Shigalyov sits in another, burning letters one by one, over a wastebasket. Marie Shatov, barefoot, with her baby in one arm, pounds on one door and then another door, throwing her weight against it.)
>	HELP ME
>	HELP ME SOMEBODY OPEN THE DOOR
>	OPEN THE DOOR
>
>	PLEASE
>	I KNOW YOU'RE IN THERE
>	OPEN THE DOOR
>	OPEN THE DOOR
>	THEY KILLED US
>	SOMEBODY HELP ME
>	THEY KILLED US

(Marie runs away. Liputin crawls around and around in a circle, as Blum kicks the daylights out of him.)

BLUM.
>TELL MEEEE

LIPUTIN.
>And Virginsky was there
>and Shigalyov too
>They were both there and they kept saying
>We should do it
>we should kill Shatov
>because Shatov was going to the Third Department

(The sound of a battering ram pounding against a door, as: Nicholas Stavrogin is packing a trunk, as Dasha stands before him.)

DASHA.
>NICHOLAS STAVROGIN
>I want you to tell me
>if you were the one who ordered Ivan's death
>If you were the one who ordered Ivan's death
>
>I cannot I ABSOLUTELY CAN NOT LIVE WITHOUT AN ANSWER
>I don't want to go to the police
>I don't want to go to the police
>I don't want to go to the police

LIPUTIN.
>I DIDN'T WANT TO DO IT
>I DIDN'T WANT TO DO IT
>I DIDN'T WANT TO DO IT

(Marie, the baby in her arms, pounding on another door.)

MARIE.
>SOMEBODY HELP ME
>HELP ME SOMEBODY
>OPEN THE DOOR

BLUM.
>TELL ME

(From outside, a battering ram slams against the door. Virginsky hides, as Shigalyov tries to brace the door.)

DASHA.
> But if you don't tell me
> I shall go mad ABSOLUTELY MAD
> Can't you see the pain I'm in
> NICHOLAS I HAVE TO KNOW

BLUM.
> TELL ME

(Virginsky runs to the door, and helps Shigalyov, as:)

MARIE.
> THEY KILLED US
> THEY KILLED US
> SOMEBODY HELP ME

DASHA.
> I AM A WOMAN GOING MAD
> I AM A WOMAN GOING MAD
> I AM A WOMAN GOING MAD

BLUM.
> TELL ME

LIPUTIN.
> PETER VERKHOVENSKY WAS THE ONE WHO DID IT
> PETER VERKHOVENSKY.
> IT WAS PETER VERKHOVENSKY FROM THE START

VIRGINSKY.
> WE'RE NOT DOGS
> YOU THINK ALL YOU HAVE TO DO IS KICK US
> AND WE'LL GO BACK TO THE KENNEL

SHIGALYOV.
> FUCK YOU
> FUCK EVERYBODY
> FUCK EVERYTHING

(The crash of the door, caving in. Wood, glass. Gunfire. More gunfire. Silence. Marie Shatov sinks to her knees in front of another door. Her breath is the loudest breath in the world. She pants and pants, her lungs filling. She sets the baby on the ground, and lowers herself onto her elbows. She still can't breathe. She tries to get lower. She rolls onto her back, suffocating.)

Scene 17

Blum stands in front of Governor Lembke. Lembke is in handcuffs. His face is covered with bruises. He is barely staying on his feet.

BLUM.
You will be put on the first available train to Moscow
There will be an officer from the Third Department traveling with you
to make sure you don't try to escape

Once you arrive
you will be remanded into the custody of the Tsar
and charged with
fraud

financial mismanagement
and general incompetence
the like of which I've never seen
You are an embarrassment to the Tsar

to me
and to your entire country
Do you have any questions
Do you have any questions

LEMBKE.
Jewish scum
(Blum takes a knife out of his pocket, and casually draws it across Lembke's hand. Lembke screams.)

Scene 18

Virginsky's face in the dark: the witness stand.

VIRGINSKY.
It started as a game of cards
We were playing cards that's all

It wasn't supposed to be political
All we were doing was talking

But if you're out of work
If somebody comes and he says
it's not fair that you're out of work
it's not fair that you can't pay your rent

or your wife is sick
or your kid died
or that other guy's got everything
while you've got nothing at all

You can't stop yourself from listening
You can't pretend you can't hear him
We're only human beings
after all

I never wanted to kill Shatov
I liked Shatov

Scene 19

Dasha stands, dressed in mourning, and watching Stavrogin drag a big black trunk down the stairs. It bangs down the stairs, step by step.

When the trunk comes to rest at the bottom of the stairs, Stavrogin takes his papers out of his pocket, and gives them to Dasha.

STAVROGIN.
 I want you to get this copied
 Don't forget
 I want it to be published in Europe too
 I've included a list of the newspapers

DASHA.
 So now it's the end

STAVROGIN.
    Nothing ever ends, Dasha

DASHA.
    You're so naive
    Everything ends
    Everything is always ending

STAVROGIN.
    Dasha Shatov
    You and your brother
    always had so much contempt for me

DASHA.
    I believed in you
    but now I can see
    I'm ten times stronger than you
    and I always will be

STAVROGIN.
    Yes you will

DASHA.
    Yes I will
    Only I think I can't marry anybody after this
    and I can't go on living here either
    Maybe I'll become a nurse
    Maybe I'll become a missionary and sell Bibles

STAVROGIN.
    Maybe you will

DASHA.
    You're going to call for me when it's over
    When nobody else wants to be with you
    When you're completely and utterly alone
    whose name will you call:

STAVROGIN.
    Dasha Shatov
    Dasha Shatov

DASHA.
> Because you can't live without me
> You just can't live without me
> Say it

STAVROGIN.
> Dasha Shatov
> Dasha Shatov

DASHA.
> Say it

STAVROGIN.
> I can't live without you
> Dasha Shatov
>
> I just can't live without you
> Dasha Shatov
>
> I can't even begin to live without you
> Dasha Shatov
> Dasha Shatov

(She turns to leave. He grabs her wrist, and pulls her back. Matryosha appears at the top of the stairs.)
> When I was in Berlin I rented
> a room in a house
> owned by a working-class couple
> They had a daughter
>
> who was 12 years old and her name was Matryosha
> It's not that Matryosha was so beautiful
> but she had this smile
> I would spend hours watching her
>
> her feet for example
> She had the most beautiful feet and wrists
> So I bought myself a notebook
> and I began to draw her
>
> in certain very favorable
> positions
> Well eventually it became clear
> that drawing her was not enough

So one afternoon
It was so easy you know
It's surprising how a thing like that
can be so easy
(Matryosha speaks from the top of the stairs.)

MATRYOSHA.
Where did you get that one

STAVROGIN.
Paris

MATRYOSHA.
This one's from Berlin
This one's from Dresden
This one's from Budapest
This one's from Lvov
and this one's from Paris

STAVROGIN.
Where's this one from

MATRYOSHA.
I forget

STAVROGIN.
Well look

MATRYOSHA.
I can't tell

STAVROGIN.
Look harder you little dunce
(Nicholas grabs Dasha and pulls her down to the floor, starting to tickle her. Dasha cries out.)

MATRYOSHA and DASHA.
Nicholas don't
Nicholas don't
Nicholas don't
(Dasha tries to escape, but he holds her. Matryosha buries her face in the stairs. She knows what's coming next. Nicholas is kissing Dasha's ears, her face, her bosom. The sound of his whispering grows and grows.)

STAVROGIN.
>Just like that yes
>Just like that
>Just like
>Mmm yes
>Soft feet
>Soft little thighs yes yes yes

(Nicholas is wetting two of his fingers in his mouth. He puts them under Dasha's dress. There is a moment of searching.)

DASHA.
>No don't
>No

(Suddenly Dasha utters a little cry of pain. Her breathing grows more rapid. He is pinning her body against himself, holding her tightly until he comes. There is a long pause, a pause longer than death. She goes limp. After a long time, Nicholas rolls off Dasha. She rolls away, and buries her face in the floor.)

STAVROGIN.
>I didn't get really scared until that night
>I was having dinner with friends
>when it suddenly occurred to me that she might tell
>>somebody
>
>her mother for example
>
>and then I was sick with fear
>I was sure I was going to prison
>I stayed out all night thinking about it
>and around dawn I began to hate her
>
>I hated her so much
>All I had to do was think of her
>and I would hate her even more
>I had such contempt for that little girl
>
>Interesting how hatred
>can win out over fear isn't it
>Around lunch time
>I began to have fantasies of killing her

So that afternoon I went back to her house
I wanted to have a fight with somebody on the way
get into a really violent fight
but I didn't

When I got there
nobody was home but Matryosha
As soon as she saw me
she started shaking her head at me

the way lower class people do
when they disapprove of someone
shaking their head
and then shaking their fist

They raise it and shake it at you
and she looked so ridiculous that way
"I killed God," she kept saying
"I killed God."

Which is exactly like a child isn't it
taking the blame for everything?
But then she did something very very strange:
she locked herself in the closet.
(Matryosha gets up, opens the closet door, goes in, and closes it behind her.)

At first I didn't know what she was going to do
I couldn't believe
a child would really do something like that
so I just sat there

The windows were open
and it was very warm
I was looking at a red spider
sitting on the leaf of a geranium
(The door grows redder and redder. Inside, Matryosha's body hangs by its neck, dead. Dasha crawls away, on her belly. Stavrogin turns and starts climbing the stairs. He falls. He gets up. He falls again. He jerks himself upright, and keeps going, as:)

I want everyone to know
I am in total control of my faculties

I'm not pleading irresponsibility or insanity
especially not insanity

If anyone wants to talk to me
I'm not going to China or anywhere else
They can find me at my mother's house
If summoned I am willing to appear anywhere
(Stavrogin drags himself into the closet. He picks up a rope, throws one end of it over a beam, and starts soaping the other end.)

Scene 20

Peter Verkhovensky at the podium, in front of a microphone.

PETER VERKHOVENSKY.
Five years ago my best friend died
I went to the funeral and I shoveled dirt on his grave
and for a while I dreamed about him all the time
He went to work with me
We drank together Ate together

We even went to the races together
And though I was always clearly aware
he was dead and buried
I was never surprised to find him at my side.
This is the way dreams are.

See this diary
In this diary he wrote down notes for a speech
he gave in 1862
None of you would know about it

It was during a certain demonstration
in a little town
that no one's ever heard of
It's about a certain mountain in China

and on this mountain
there lives a group of people

who are completely unafraid
Their eyes are bright

Their faces are full of intelligence
and yet they are innocent
because they live on a mountain
where there is no such thing as sin
and their children are all common children

and together they form one common family
and there is no disease on this mountain either
only noble peaceful death
and there are no churches or temples or mosques
There is no religion at all

because these people no longer
have to earn their places in Paradise
They already live in Paradise
It was a pretty good speech
It was a speech about civilization

When I heard it I thought
you're right life is terrible
but if we could work together
we could civilize the world
ALL IT TAKES IS WORK

Now I'm old
I live alone
I have no friends
and no money
and nothing has changed:

The rich are still sucking the blood of the poor
The politicians are still sitting around
with their arms folded
talking about civilization
as our old people starve
our prophets are murdered
and our children devour each other
like wolves

(Stavrogin gets up on a stool, and throws the other end over a beam. He ties it off. He steps off the stool. His legs kick. After a moment, they stop kicking.)

And so I have given up civilization.

I am no longer willing to
discuss civilization
I am no longer willing to read books about civilization

and I am not
I am especially not
willing to listen to the lectures of intellectuals
who are busily planning for civilization
a thousand years hence

while the meat
which should be feeding our children now
is flying into the mouths of our despots
Don't tell me about civilization
while despots are taking over my supper table
eating my meals
and drinking my drink

It's justice that will make me happy not civilization
It's justice that will make me equal
not priests or politicians
Ladies and gentlemen
I have given up civilization

because I prefer the quicker path
of slitting a million throats NOW
instead of waiting to slit 500 million throats
A HUNDRED YEARS FROM NOW

If nothing else
they shall remember us by the sound of our screaming:

GIVE US JUSTICE
GIVE US JUSTICE
GIVE US JUSTICE
GIVE US JUSTICE
GIVE US JUSTICE

Scene 21

Dasha writes a letter.

DASHA.
Dear friend
I am writing you this letter
from my new country
where there are more birds than I can name
I am learning a whole new language
I have a palm tree outside my window
and every morning
I can see all the way to Gibraltar
and there are no tears here

(*Meanwhile*: Mrs. Stavrogin *starts taking down her hair, pulling out pin after pin, as:*)

Last night I had another dream about him
In the dream he was very close to me
I could feel his breath
his hand upon my heart

We were all standing on the roof
You and him and me and even my brother
and the sun was shining

and down in the street
people were playing
Everyone was so happy

Everyone was
And in the summer house
the roses were

so fragile
always and forever fragile

(*Mrs. Stavrogin's long hair tumbles down her back. It is grey, yellow and lifeless. It reaches all the way to her knees.*)

Right now what I am going to do is sleep for an hour
une heure

(A drum rattles. <u>Go To</u>: three men being shoved in front of a wall. They are Virginsky, Shigalyov, and Liputin. Hoods are pulled over their heads, as:)

BLUM'S VOICE.
    READY

DASHA'S VOICE.
    and then I shall drink a glass of tea
    un verre de the

BLUM'S VOICE.
    AIM

DASHA'S VOICE.
    et enfin je serai tres heureuse
    and then at last I shall be very happy

BLUM'S VOICE.
    FIRE

(A round of gunfire.)

THE END

PROPERTY LIST

Playing cards
Briefcase with letter (PETER VERKHOVENSKY)
Printing plate (PETER VERKHOVENSKY, SHATOV)
Laundry basket (DASHA)
Wallet with money (bills) (LIPUTIN)
Pair of dumbbells
Teapot with tea (KIRILOV)
Tea cups with saucers (KIRILOV)
Tray with sugar (PETER VERKHOVENSKY)
Flask (LIPUTIN)
Printing roller (SHATOV)
Printing press (SHATOV)
Travel trunk with items (MRS. STAVROGIN)
Letter (STEPAN VERKHOVENSKY)
Letter (MRS. LEMBKE)
Wallet with money (bills) (LEMBKE)
Envelope
Portfolio with posters (SHATOV)
Tin dishes (SHATOV)
Toy train (LEMBKE)
Toy village (LEMBKE)
Tall pile of linen (DASHA)
Buckets (DASHA)
Checkbook (MRS. STAVROGIN)
Pistol (KIRILOV)
Cigarette (PETER VERKHOVENSKY)
Matches (PETER VERKHOVENSKY)
Gun (PETER VERKHOVENSKY)
Bullets (PETER VERKHOVENSKY)
Poster (SHIGALYOV, VIRGINSKY, LIPUTIN)
Nails (SHIGALYOV, VIRGINSKY, LIPUTIN)
Posters (STEPAN VERKHOVENSKY, MRS. LEMBKE)
Listening device (LEMBKE)
Tray with tea, bread, cheese (KIRILOV)
Makeup (MRS. STAVROGIN)

Pen (NICHOLAS STAVROGIN)
Paper (NICHOLAS STAVROGIN)
Poultices (STEPAN VERKHOVENSKY,
  MRS. STAVROGIN)
Handkerchief (MRS. STAVROGIN
Canister of liquid (SHIGALYOV)
Small flasks (SHIGALYOV)
Rag (SHIGALYOV)
Bottle (SHIGALYOV)
Match (SHIGALYOV)
Stockings (MRS. LEMBKE)
Jump rope (MATRYOSHA)
Empty plate (LIPUTIN)
Bottle of champagne (BLUM)
Necklace of daisies (LEMBKE)
Handcuffs (BLUM)
Champagne glass (MRS. LEMBKE)
Checkbook (MRS. STAVROGIN)
Pen (MRS. STAVROGIN)
Basket with laundry (DASHA)
Bread (SHATOV)
Bag of supplies (SHATOV)
Purse with comb (DASHA)
Loaf of bread (KIRILOV)
Knife (KIRILOV)
Lanterns (KIRILOV, SHIGALYOV, LIPUTIN,
  PETER VERKHOVENSKY)
Match (KIRILOV)
Baby (DASHA)
Rags (DASHA)
2 large stones (LIPUTIN, SHIGALYOV)
Ropes (VIRGINSKY, PETER VERKHOVENSKY)
Candles, lit (MRS. STAVROGIN, PETER
  VERKHOVENSKY)
Gun (KIRILOV)
Pen (KIRILOV)
Paper (KIRILOV)
Matches (PETER VERKHOVENSKY)

Wastebasket with fire (SHIGALYOV)
Letters (SHIGALYOV)
Knife (BLUM)
Papers (STAVROGIN)
Rope (STAVROGIN)
Soap (STAVROGIN)
Hair pins (MRS. STAVROGIN)

SOUND EFFECTS

Glacier shifting
Wood straining
Glass creaking
Water dripping
Doors slamming
Footsteps down a flight of stairs
Factory machinery
Doorbell
Big dog barking
Factory sounds
Running
Furniture turning over
Glass breaking
Shelves and books falling
Flock of birds taking flight
100 people dancing to a polka
Gloved applause
Glasses clinking
Murmuring
Rain on roof
Fire bells distant
Fire wagon with bells and horns
Distant explosion
Explosion
Flames crackling
Crashing of a door caving in
Gunfire

NEW PLAYS

- **MERE MORTALS** by David Ives, author of *All in the Timing*. Another critically acclaimed evening of one-act comedies combining wit, satire, hilarity and intellect -- a winning combination. The entire evening of plays can be performed by 3 men and 3 women. ISBN: 0-8222-1632-9

- **BALLAD OF YACHIYO** by Philip Kan Gotanda. A provocative play about innocence, passion and betrayal, set against the backdrop of a Hawaiian sugar plantation in the early 1900s. *"Gotanda's writing is superb ... a great deal of fine craftsmanship on display here, and much to enjoy."* --*Variety*. *"...one of the country's most consistently intriguing playwrights..."* --*San Francisco Examiner*. *"As he has in past plays, Gotanda defies expectations..."* --*Oakland Tribune*. [3M, 4W] ISBN: 0-8222-1547-0

- **MINUTES FROM THE BLUE ROUTE** by Tom Donaghy. While packing up a house, a family converges for a weekend of flaring tempers and shattered illusions. *"With MINUTES FROM THE BLUE ROUTE [Donaghy] succeeds not only in telling a story -- a typically American one with wide appeal, about how parents and kids struggle to understand each other and mostly fail -- but in noting it inventively, through wittily elliptical, crisscrossed speeches, and in making it carry a fairly vast amount of serious weight with surprising ease."* --*Village Voice*. [2M, 2W] ISBN: 0-8222-1608-6

- **SCAPIN** by Molière, adapted by Bill Irwin and Mark O'Donnell. This adaptation of Molière's 325-year-old farce, *Les Fourberies de Scapin*, keeps the play in period while adding a late Twentieth Century spin to the language and action. *"This SCAPIN, [with a] felicitous adaptation by Mark O'Donnell, would probably have gone over big with the same audience who first saw Molière's Fourberies de Scapin...in Paris in 1671."* --*N.Y. Times*. *"Commedia dell'arte and vaudeville have at least two things in common: baggy pants and Bill Irwin. All make for a natural fit in the celebrated clown's entirely unconventional adaptation."* --*Variety* [9M, 3W, flexible] ISBN: 0-8222-1603-5

- **THE TURN OF THE SCREW** adapted for the stage by Jeffrey Hatcher from the story by Henry James. The American master's classic tale of possession is given its most interesting "turn" yet: one woman plays the mansion's terrified governess while a single male actor plays everyone else. *"In his thoughtful adaptation of Henry James' spooky tale, Jeffrey Hatcher does away with the supernatural flummery, exchanging the story's balanced ambiguities about the nature of reality for a portrait of psychological vampirism..."* --*Boston Globe*. [1M, 1W] ISBN: 0-8222-1554-3

- **NEVILLE'S ISLAND** by Tim Firth. A middle management orientation exercise turns into an hilarious disaster when the team gets "shipwrecked" on an uninhabited island. *"NEVILLE'S ISLAND ... is that rare event: a genuinely good new play..., it's a comedic, adult LORD OF THE FLIES..."* --*The Guardian*. *"... A non-stop, whitewater deluge of comedy both sophisticated and slapstick.... Firth takes a perfect premise and shoots it to the extreme, flipping his fish out of water, watching them flop around a bit, and then masterminding the inevitable feeding frenzy."* --*New Mexican*. [4M] ISBN: 0-8222-1581-0

DRAMATISTS PLAY SERVICE, INC.
440 Park Avenue South, New York, NY 10016 212-683-8960 Fax 212-213-1539
postmaster@dramatists.com www.dramatists.com

NEW PLAYS

- **TAKING SIDES by Ronald Harwood.** Based on the true story of one of the world's greatest conductors whose wartime decision to remain in Germany brought him under the scrutiny of a U.S. Army determined to prove him a Nazi. *"A brave, wise and deeply moving play delineating the confrontation between culture, and power, between art and politics, between irresponsible freedom and responsible compromise." --London Sunday Times.* [4M, 3W] ISBN: 0-8222-1566-7

- **MISSING/KISSING by John Patrick Shanley.** Two biting short comedies, MISSING MARISA and KISSING CHRISTINE, by one of America's foremost dramatists and the Academy Award winning author of *Moonstruck*. *"... Shanley has an unusual talent for situations ... and a sure gift for a kind of inner dialogue in which people talk their hearts as well as their minds...." --N.Y. Post.* MISSING MARISA [2M], KISSING CHRISTINE [1M, 2W] ISBN: 0-8222-1590-X

- **THE SISTERS ROSENSWEIG by Wendy Wasserstein,** Pulitzer Prize-winning author of *The Heidi Chronicles*. Winner of the 1993 Outer Critics Circle Award for Best Broadway Play. A captivating portrait of three disparate sisters reuniting after a lengthy separation on the eldest's 50th birthday. *"The laughter is all but continuous." --New Yorker. "Funny. Observant. A play with wit as well as acumen.... In dealing with social and cultural paradoxes, Ms. Wasserstein is, as always, the most astute of commentators." --N.Y. Times.* [4M, 4W] ISBN: 0-8222-1348-6

- **MASTER CLASS by Terrence McNally. Winner of the 1996 Tony Award for Best Play.** Only a year after winning the Tony Award for *Love! Valour! Compassion!*, Terrence McNally scores again with the most celebrated play of the year, an unforgettable portrait of Maria Callas, our century's greatest opera diva. *"One of the white-hot moments of contemporary theatre. A total triumph." --N.Y. Post. "Blazingly theatrical." -- USA Today.* [3M, 3W] ISBN: 0-8222-1521-7

- **DEALER'S CHOICE by Patrick Marber.** A weekly poker game pits a son addicted to gambling against his own father, who also has a problem but won't admit it. *"... make tracks to DEALER'S CHOICE, Patrick Marber's wonderfully masculine, razor-sharp dissection of poker-as-life.... It's a play that comes out swinging and never lets up -- a witty, wisecracking drama that relentlessly probes the tortured souls of its six very distinctive ... characters. CHOICE is a cutthroat pleasure that you won't want to miss." --Time Out (New York).* [6M] ISBN: 0-8222-1616-7

- **RIFF RAFF by Laurence Fishburne.** RIFF RAFF marks the playwriting debut of one of Hollywood's most exciting and versatile actors. *"Mr. Fishburne is surprisingly and effectively understated, with scalding bubbles of anxiety breaking through the surface of a numbed calm." --N.Y. Times. "Fishburne has a talent and a quality...[he] possesses one of the vital requirements of a playwright -- a good ear for the things people say and the way they say them." --N.Y. Post.* [3M] ISBN: 0-8222-1545-4

DRAMATISTS PLAY SERVICE, INC.
440 Park Avenue South, New York, NY 10016 212-683-8960 Fax 212-213-1539
postmaster@dramatists.com www.dramatists.com